Recipes from the
PACIFIC RIM

Recipes from the
PACIFIC RIM

REGIONAL SPECIALITIES FROM
THE WEST COAST OF AMERICA,
MEXICO AND HAWAII

Marjie Lambert

APPLE

A QUINTET BOOK

PUBLISHED BY THE APPLE PRESS
6 BLUNDELL STREET
LONDON N7 9BH

ISBN 1-85076-595-2

This book was designed and produced
by Quintet Publishing Limited
6 Blundell Street
London N7 9BH

Creative Director: Richard Dewing
Designer: Fiona Roberts
Project Editor: Anna Briffa
Editor: Susan Martineau
Photographer: Andrew Sydenham
Food Stylist: Sunil Vijayakar

Typeset in Great Britain by
Central Southern Typesetters, Eastbourne
Manufactured in Malaysia by
C.H. Colour Scan Sdn. Bhd.
Printed in Singapore by
Star Standard Industries (Pte) Ltd

AUTHOR'S DEDICATION & ACKNOWLEDGEMENTS
Dedicated to friends who have stuck with me for more than
20 years and across great distances: to Michelle and Anne-Marie,
who baked cookies with me when we were children; to Rick
who gave me my first wok and introduced me to Thai food; and
to Lynda, who taught me how to make spanikopita.

ACKNOWLEDGEMENTS:
With thanks to Laura, Vicki and Terry for their continuing
support, and to Helen, Anna and Laura at Quintet.

CONTENTS

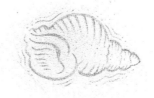

*Pacific Rim cooking encompasses the various regional cuisines
of the west coast of North America, all the way from Mexico to Alaska,
plus Hawaii and Tahiti. The combinations spill over and influence
each other, creating new dishes which pull together styles and
ingredients from a host of different cultures.*

INTRODUCTION

INTRODUCTION

I grew up in Los Angeles, where my neighbours and schoolmates were from Bolivia, Armenia, China, Mexico, Germany, Poland, Japan and the Philippines. The kitchens I ran through as a child smelled of exotic dishes that I was always eager to taste and – when I was older – to cook. The food was a shifting jumble of ingredients and dishes that changed whenever new neighbours arrived. Pacific Rim cooking is like that – not a well-defined cuisine but one that adapts to the ethnic influences of the neighbours.

Pacific Rim cooking encompasses the cuisines of the west coast of North America, from Mexico to Alaska, plus Hawaii and Tahiti. It is a combination of varied regional cuisines that spill over and influence each other, always creating new dishes that pull together styles and ingredients from different cultures.

Those regional cuisines are linked by their use of the fruits of the Pacific, the wealth of fish and shellfish that are fished from the warm waters off Mexico to the frigid waters of Alaska. But their distinctive cooking styles are often marked by how they use the fruits of the field. In Pacific Rim cooking, fish may be seasoned with chillies, lime juice, sun-dried tomatoes, basil vinaigrette, mango salsa, blueberry chutney or roasted macadamia nuts.

The Pacific region is a region of abundance. The orange groves and onion fields that once stood at the edge of Los Angeles have been uprooted and ploughed under to make way for thousands of new homes, but it is only 100 miles (160km) from my childhood home to the Imperial Valley fields planted with lettuce and melons, or the fruit orchards of the San Joaquin Valley. California, Oregon and Washington are the source of much of the nation's fresh produce. Even Alaska, with its short summers and long months of below-freezing temperatures, produces berries, wild greens and wild mushrooms.

Pacific Rim cooking began with the American Indians, the Aleuts, the Eskimos, the Polynesians and the other native peoples who lived in these lands before white settlers. Their staples – including ground corn, roasted or dried salmon, dried fruits and berries, nuts ground into meal – remain an important part of cooking today. How each area's cuisine developed depended in part on what fruits and vegetables thrived in its climate, and in part on the culture of the immigrants who settled there.

Mexican cooking is distinctive for its use of chillies, tropical fruits and ground corn, which can be made into tortillas and tamales. Yet Mexican cooking is far more varied and creative than the tacos, enchiladas and burritos that are so familiar outside the country. In Mexico's Pacific region, a whole fish might be stuffed with vegetables, wrapped in corn tortillas and barbecued. Dried prawns and corn tortilla masa are made into fritters. Shredded pork is mixed with pinto beans, served over fried chillies, and topped with mole sauce. Chicken livers are fried with smokey chipotle chillies.

To the north, California cuisine is distinctive because of the enormous variety of fresh produce grown there, from the avocado groves of San Diego to the rice paddies of the Sacramento Valley, the pomegranate orchards of the San Joaquin Valley, the strawberry fields of Watsonville, and the asparagus farms in the Sacramento River Delta. California's dairy industry is growing and producing more speciality cheeses. And California's rich immigrant mix, larger than any other state in the U.S., has had an enormous influence on how those foods are prepared. Its largest immigrant groups are from Latin America and Asia, with smaller populations from dozens of other countries. California cuisine might be a soup of Pacific prawns simmered in coconut milk and flavoured with coriander and lemongrass. Warm

artichoke hearts tossed with fresh goats' cheese and pine nuts. Grilled salmon served with a salsa of black beans, corn and chillies.

Immigration has influenced the cuisine of the Pacific Northwest as well, from the Basque settlements of eastern Oregon, to the Scandinavian neighbourhoods of Washington's Puget Sound and the Asian immigrants of Vancouver, British Columbia. The valleys of Oregon, Washington and British Columbia produce a wealth of fruits, nuts and berries. The fishing industry has been battered by recession, environmental restrictions and pollution, but remains an important factor in the cuisine. Oregon and Washington, too, are producing more speciality cheeses. Cuisine from the Pacific Northwest might include wonton wrappers stuffed with crab, a spinach salad topped with mussels, hazelnuts and Walla Walla sweet onions, roast duck with apples, and warm shortcake smothered with blackberries, raspberries and strawberries.

More than other Pacific Rim cuisines, Alaskan cooking relies on hunting and fishing. Modern refrigeration and transportation have made imported foods more accessible, but fish and game remain staples. Because of its climate, Alaska does not have the variety of locally grown produce that milder climates enjoy. Its only tree fruit is the crab apple, but blueberries, raspberries, cranberries, cloudberries, salmonberries and tiny strawberries grow wild. Gold miners brought sourdough bread to Alaska. Russian immigrants introduced gardening, although the growing season is short. Alaskan cuisine might include salmon stuffed with wild mushrooms, halibut served on a bed of wild greens, venison steak and blueberry chutney, and sourdough bread made with whale oil.

Tahiti and the Hawaiian Islands also rely on seafood, but of the warmwater variety. Some non-native fish and shellfish are farmed. The islands grow a rich variety of produce that may seem extremely exotic to

WONTON CRISPS

makes 60–135 crisps, depending on size

Wonton or eggroll wrappers, now available in the chiller cabinet or oriental department of many supermarkets, are easy to work with. In addition to making excellent wrappers, they can be fried until crisp and eaten like potato crisps. Try them with Apricot Dipping Sauce (page 22) or Salsa (page 29). (See notes on Deep-frying, right.)

450g/1 lb wonton or eggroll wrappers
oil for deep-frying

~ Most wonton wrappers are about 7.5 cm/3 in square and do not need to be cut. Eggroll wrappers are about 15 cm/6 in square and should be cut into thirds crossways and lengthways, to make 9 crisps per sheet. Since the pastry dries out quickly, it is better to wait until just before frying to cut and separate them. Keep them covered with a barely damp teatowel when you're not working with them.
~ Pour oil 2.5–5 cm/1–2 in deep in a frying pan or other heavy pan. Heat oil to 185°C/365°F, then reduce heat so the temperature doesn't continue to rise.
~ Carefully add a few crisps to the oil and make sure they don't stick to each other. Fry the crisps until they're golden brown, 30 to 40 seconds. Leave them to drain on kitchen paper towels. Make sure oil temperature has not dropped before frying the next batch.
~ The crisps are best eaten warm, but are also good cold.

DEEP-FRYING

Deep-frying can be messy and intimidating. Here are some tricks to keep it from being that way – and to avoid greasy or burnt food.

The biggest mistake people make in deep-frying is not having the oil at the proper temperature. Too hot and it instantly blackens the outside and leaves the inside raw; not hot enough and the food absorbs a lot of extra grease while it cooks. That's why a thermometer is critical.

But you also need patience. Every time you add food to the oil, the temperature of the oil drops. Wait for the oil to come back up to the proper temperature before frying the next batch, and then make sure the temperature doesn't keep rising.

You also need to be familiar with how quickly your cooker heats oil. Once it's hot, the temperature can climb rapidly. You need to know at what setting it will hold the same temperature, then how high to set it when it's time to reheat the oil for the next batch of food. Most food fries best at about 185°C/365°F, but on my electric cooker, the oil gets too hot, too fast. I have my best luck frying at between 170° and 175°C/340° and 350°F. Start by frying a single item of food and watching how quickly it cooks.

Deep-frying can be dangerous. The hot oil will splatter if it comes in contact with water or other liquids, and can cause a nasty burn. Wear oven mitts that cover at least your hands and wrists, and use long-handled tongs.

The best oils for deep-frying are vegetable or peanut oil or solid vegetable fat. Do not use olive oil or butter.

LOMI LOMI SALMON

makes 4 servings

Lomi Lomi salmon is the Hawaiian version of Mexican ceviche. Fish – in this case salmon – is marinated for a day in lime juice, which "cooks" the flesh without heat. Look for very fresh, high-quality salmon. Lomi Lomi salmon can be served over ice like a prawn cocktail, over lettuce as a salad, or stuffed in hollowed-out cherry tomatoes. For an extra kick, add a finely chopped jalapeño chilli.

225 g/8 oz high-quality salmon, skinned
120 ml/4 fl oz fresh lime juice
1 tsp sugar
2 tomatoes, seeded and chopped
½ red pepper, seeded and diced
2 spring onions, chopped
salt and pepper to taste
1 finely chopped jalapeño chilli, optional

~ Put the salmon in a non-reactive dish. Pour the lime juice over it. Turn the salmon to be sure all sides are coated with lime juice. Sprinkle both sides lightly with sugar. Leave the salmon to marinate, refrigerated, at least 12 hours, until the deep red colour disappears. Spoon lime juice over the fish occasionally.
~ Drain the fish. Shred the fish with your fingers, checking for any bones. Mix the shredded fish with the chopped vegetables, then add salt and pepper to taste and the chilli if using.

Lomi Lomi Salmon ➤

APPETIZERS

With influences from the Far East and Europe as well as traditions
from Mexico and California, the variety in this selection offers a host of exotic
flavours: Hoisin sauce, coriander, ginger and jalapeño are just a few.

mainlanders but are staples to islanders. Green mangoes and papayas may be eaten as vegetables, while guavas and passion fruit are eaten as casually as peaches are on the mainland. Food may be steamed in banana or taro leaves. Like the rest of the Pacific region, Tahitian and Hawaiian cuisines have been influenced by immigrants. Most of those immigrants are from Southeast Asia, but Portuguese settlers also had an impact on island cuisine. Roast pork might be served with pineapple salsa. Fillets of wahoo or mahi mahi might be dipped in ground macadamia nuts and served with papaya butter. Sweet Hawaiian crabmeat might be tossed with pasta and a ginger-scented cream sauce.

Yet as soon as we try to define Pacific Rim cooking, the definition becomes obsolete. Hawaii didn't have locally grown tomatoes a few years ago. Now chefs can turn to their local suppliers instead of shipping in tomatoes from the mainland. Farmers are experimenting with mango groves in California. The relatively new Laotian and Vietnamese immigrant populations have introduced their cuisine into the mix – lemongrass, almost unknown in the U.S. a decade ago, is now available in many West Coast stores. Technology, such as the pasta machine, has brought gourmet food into more kitchens.

That is one of the joys of Pacific Rim cooking. It is always changing, finding new ingredients and new ways to use old standards. In that spirit, perhaps this cookbook can serve as a map, giving you not just the recipes printed on these pages, but guiding you toward your own Pacific Rim creations.

SPRING ROLLS

makes 15 spring rolls

—

*Spring rolls are a Vietnamese dish, similar to a Chinese eggroll, made with pork or
a combination of pork and seafood, bean thread noodles, and a mix of vegetables and herbs.
(See notes on Deep-frying, page 14.) Traditionally, spring rolls are made with rice paper
wrappers, but this recipe calls for eggroll wrappers because they are more readily available.
Eggroll wrappers should be about 15 cm/6 in square. Bean thread noodles are a very fine,
cellophane-looking noodle made from mung beans. They are available in Chinese food shops
and in the Oriental food section of better-stocked supermarkets. Jicama is a white-fleshed tuber
known as yam bean or bangkwang. Also used in Mexican dishes, it is widely available. However,
if you can't find it, substitute bean sprouts and/or chopped water chestnuts. Many spring roll
recipes use dried mushrooms and a dried black fungus called tree ears. If you can find them,
soak them in warm water until they are soft, then chop them and add to the filling.
You can also substitute crab or prawns for part of the pork. The traditional
dipping sauce for spring rolls is a garlicky sweet-sour sauce made with fish sauce.
Since fish sauce is not easy to find outside Oriental food shops, substitute Apricot Dipping
Sauce (page 22) or bought Chinese hot mustard and soy sauce.*

1½ oz/40 g bean thread noodles
225 g/8 oz lean minced pork
50 g/2 oz onion, chopped
25 g/1 oz carrot, grated
50 g/2 oz jicama, cut into strips
40 g/1½ oz mushrooms, chopped
1 clove garlic, crushed
2 tbsp chopped fresh coriander
1 tsp grated fresh ginger
½ tsp salt
pinch of black pepper
15 eggroll wrappers (about 450 g/1 lb)
oil for deep-frying

~ Put the bean thread noodles in a bowl and cover them with warm water. Leave them for 30 minutes until they are soft. Drain the noodles well and cut them into 2.5-cm/1-in lengths.

~ Mix the noodles with the pork, onion, carrot, jicama, mushrooms, garlic, coriander, ginger, salt and pepper.

~ Peel off an eggroll wrapper. Keep the remaining wrappers covered with a damp teatowel so they don't dry out. Lightly brush water around the edges of the wrapper. Place about 2 tablespoons of filling a little above the centre of the wrapper. Shape it into a line about 10 cm/4 in long, leaving about 2.5 cm/1 in of wrapper on either side. Starting from the top, roll down the wrapper. When it is rolled past the filling, fold over the sides and press down the edges to seal. Continue rolling until it is a cylinder. Press the bottom edge to seal. Set aside spring roll and repeat process with another wrapper.

~ Pour oil in a large pan 7.5–10 cm/3–4 in deep. Heat to 175°C/350°F, then reduce heat so the temperature of the oil doesn't continue to rise.

~ Start by putting just one spring roll into the hot oil. It will puff up and rise to the surface. Hold it under the oil, otherwise the top won't cook evenly. Cook until the roll is golden brown, 2½ to 3 minutes. Remove it from the oil and let it drain. Cut it open to be sure pork is cooked – it should have lost any sign of pink.

~ Make any needed adjustments to the temperature of the oil. Cook spring rolls, a few at a time so they do not crowd each other.

ONION-CHILLI FLAN

makes 6 servings
—

*Slow-cooked onions, chillies, and Monterey Jack cheese are
a delicious combination in this appetizer. Use Maui or
Walla Walla sweet onions if they're available.*

*25 g/1 oz butter
2 large yellow onions
2 poblano or Anaheim chillies, or 3 jalapeños
23-cm/9-in pie crust, part baked
225 g/8 oz Monterey Jack or Cheddar cheese, grated
3 eggs, lightly beaten with a fork
120 ml/4 fl oz soured cream
120 ml/4 fl oz milk
¼ tsp ground cumin
¼ tsp white pepper
½ tsp salt
sliced avocado for garnish*

~ Slice the onions, then cut the slices in half and
separate the rings. Melt the butter in a large
frying pan. Add the onions and sauté over low
heat until they are golden, 20–25 minutes.

~ While the onions are cooking, prepare the
chillies. If using poblano or Anaheim chillies,
roast them (see notes on Roasting Chillies, page
26), then peel, seed and chop them. Jalapeño
chillies can be used raw for a sharper bite, or
roasted and peeled for a more mellow flavour.
~ Preheat the oven to 180°C/350°F/Gas Mark 4.
~ When the onions are ready, mix in the
chillies, then put the onion-chilli mixture in the
part baked pastry base. Sprinkle grated cheese
over the onions.
~ Make a custard by combining the remaining
ingredients except the avocados. Pour the
custard over the onions and cheese. Bake until
custard is set and lightly brown, 40–45 minutes.
Leave to cool slightly, then serve warm,
garnished with avocado slices.

PASTRY CASE
for a 23-cm/9-in pastry case
—

*150 g/5 oz plain flour
¼ tsp salt
50 g/2 oz lard or vegetable fat
50 g/2 oz butter, chilled
about 45 ml/3 tbsp iced water*

~ Combine the flour and salt. Using a pastry
cutter or sharp knife, cut in the lard and butter
until the mixture has a coarse grain and tiny bits
of fat remain. Sprinkle the iced water over the
mixture, 15 ml/1 tbsp at a time, until the dough
forms a ball, but is not sticky. You may also do
this in a food processor, but use a very light
touch or the dough will be tough. Mix in the
water by hand so you can feel when it's ready.
~ The dough will be easier to handle if you
wrap the ball in cling film and refrigerate it for
20–30 minutes.
~ Roll out the dough on a lightly floured
surface to about 28 cm/11 in in diameter. If you
have rolled out the dough on waxed paper,
invert the flan tin and centre it over the dough.
Next, invert the dough and flan tin at the same
time. Peel the paper off the dough and lightly
press it into the tin. If the dough is not on
greaseproof paper, carefully fold it in quarters.
Place it in the flan tin and unfold. Trim the
dough to a 2.5-cm/1-in overhang. Roll up the
overhang and pinch into a fluted edge. The
dough will have a flakier texture if it is
refrigerated 20 minutes or longer before baking.
~ For recipes that require a pre-baked case, bake
in a preheated 200°C/400°F/Gas Mark 6 oven
until lightly browned, 12 to 14 minutes. Then
proceed with chosen recipe.

WALNUT AND BLUE CHEESE SPREAD

makes about 250 g/9 oz

This easy-to-make spread, served on crackers, is excellent with red wine or port. Use any kind of blue cheese – Stilton, Roquefort or Gorgonzola. If the blue cheese is too pungent, add a little more cream cheese. The spread is best if made in advance and allowed to stand, refrigerated, overnight. The secret to excellent flavour and easy spreading is to serve it at room temperature.

175 g/6 oz blue cheese, crumbled, at room temperature
75 g/3 oz cream cheese, softened to room temperature
30 ml/2 tbsp brandy
75 g/3 oz walnuts, chopped

~ Put the cheese and brandy in a blender or food processor and blend until smooth. Stir in walnuts.

CROSTINI

makes about 40 pieces

Crostini refers to the toasted bread that is the base for this finger food. It is particularly popular in San Francisco, where the cuisine was strongly influenced by Italian immigrants. The tomato-olive salsa should be made several hours, or as much as a day, in advance. Look for fresh mozzarella. The bland pre-packaged mozzarella available in some supermarkets won't stand up to the competing flavours.

1 large red pepper
2 baguettes French bread, each cut into about 20 slices
1 large or 2 small tomatoes, peeled, seeded and chopped
3 garlic cloves, crushed
1 x 75-g/3-oz can of black olives, drained and coarsely chopped
1 jalapeño chilli, seeds included, finely chopped
about 8 anchovy fillets, finely chopped
2 tbsp chopped fresh basil
¼ tsp dried oregano
2 tbsp olive oil
¼ tsp pepper
salt to taste
300–350 g/10–12 oz fresh mozzarella, thinly sliced

~ Preheat the grill.
~ Rinse the pepper, cut into 4 fairly flat pieces, and trim seeds and membranes. Place the pieces under the grill, skin side up. Grill until skin is blistered and mostly black. Remove the peppers from grill and place in a plastic bag to steam for 10 minutes.
~ Cut the baguette into 1 cm/½-in slices. Put the bread on a grill pan and grill, turning once, until golden on both sides.
~ Peel the skin from the pepper and chop the pepper. Put the pepper in a bowl with the tomatoes, garlic, olives, jalapeño, anchovy, basil, oregano, olive oil and pepper. Mix ingredients. Taste and salt if necessary. Because of the saltiness of the anchovies, it may not need any salt. This salsa improves after flavours have been allowed to blend for several hours.
~ Spoon a little tomato mixture on each slice of bread, avoiding the watery juices that will have collected in the salsa. Top with a thin slice of mozzarella cheese. Grill until cheese is bubbly. Serve immediately.

CORIANDER CHEESE BITES

makes 50–60 turnovers

Made with coriander pesto, ricotta cheese and filo dough, these savoury turnovers are a popular party dish. They can be assembled in advance, refrigerated, then baked at the last minute. See notes on Working with Filo, right, if you've never cooked with filo.

*450 g/1 lb ricotta cheese
about 50 g/2 oz coriander leaves
2 cloves garlic, peeled
1/4 of a medium onion
15 ml/1 tbsp olive oil
40 g/1½ oz walnuts
½ tsp salt
1 lb/450g filo (about 20 sheets)
butter-flavour vegetable spray, optional
50 g/2 oz butter, melted*

~ Preheat the oven to 170°C/325°F/Gas Mark 3. Line some baking sheets with foil.
~ Put the ricotta cheese in a mixing bowl, then tilt the bowl so any liquids can drain. This will keep the filling from being runny. Allow the cheese to drain like this for 20 minutes or so, then carefully pour off any liquids.
~ Put the coriander, garlic, onion, olive oil, walnuts and salt in the food processor. Process until mixture is coarsely textured, but not a smooth paste. Mix this pesto with the ricotta cheese.
~ Peel off a sheet of filo dough. Cover the rest with a damp teatowel to keep it from drying out. Spray the filo with vegetable spray, taking care to spray the edges. Alternatively, brush with melted butter. Cut the sheets into thirds across its width. Fold each third in half along its length, so you have 3 narrow strips.
~ Place 2–3 teaspoons of filling at the top of the first strip. Fold the corner diagonally across the filling. Continue folding like a flag into a triangle until you get to the end of the strip. Lightly brush outside with melted butter, especially at the end of the filo. Place turnover on baking sheet. Repeat process until you've used up the filling or the filo.
~ Bake the turnovers until golden, about 10 minutes. Leave to cool slightly – the hot cheese can burn your mouth – but serve while they are warm.

WORKING WITH FILO

Filo is a thin, fragile pastry dough frequently used in Greek foods, including baklava and spanikopita. Although it can be difficult to work with, it is worth learning how to handle because of its versatility and delicious uses.

Filo, usually purchased frozen, should be thawed in the refrigerator before using. Its moisture must be maintained. It dries out quickly if unprotected and becomes brittle. If it gets wet, it falls apart. When cooking with filo, use a barely damp teatowel to cover the sheets of dough you're not working with at that minute, to keep them from drying out. Most recipes require the filo to be brushed with melted butter. However, it's easy to use too much butter, and make the filo soggy. One alternative is to spray each sheet with a butter-flavoured cooking spray, if available.

If you use the filo to make turnovers – for example, the Coriander Cheese Bites (left) – a wet filling can make the turnovers fall apart. Reduce the filling's liquid ingredients as much as possible. Use a cooking spray instead of butter, brushing melted butter on the turnovers only to seal the edges. And, if necessary, use two sheets of filo instead of one.

CRAB WONTONS

makes about 60

---

*Wonton or eggroll wrappers, now widely available, are wrapped around a
savoury crab filling and deep-fried. This crisp and delicious appetizer can be served with
Apricot Dipping Sauce (recipe follows) or with Chinese hot mustard and soy sauce.
(See notes on Deep-frying, page 14.)*

*175 g/6 oz crabmeat, picked over for bits of shell
40 g/1½ oz water chestnuts, chopped
3 spring onions, white part only, finely chopped
1 clove garlic, crushed
15 ml/1 tbsp vegetable oil
45 ml/3 tbsp milk or single cream
¼ tsp salt
450 g/1 lb wonton wrappers (about 60) or eggroll
wrappers
oil for deep-frying*

~ Mix the crabmeat, water chestnuts, spring onions, garlic, vegetable oil, milk or cream and salt.

~ Peel off a wonton wrapper. (Eggroll wrappers are the same as wonton wrappers, only larger. They usually measure about 15 cm/6 in square, and should be quartered to be used as wonton wrappers.) Cover remaining wrappers with a damp teatowel. Lightly brush edges of wrapper with water. Put 1 teaspoon crab filling in centre of wonton. The wrapper can be folded in half diagonally, and its edges pressed together. Or, you can bring the edges up, gather them into a pouch-like shape, and press the gathers together. Wetting the edges helps seal them. Repeat until you have used up the wrappers and filling.

~ Pour oil 5–7.5 cm/2–3 in deep in a large frying pan or heavy pan. Heat oil to 185°C/365°F, then reduce heat so oil temperature doesn't keep rising. Test by putting a single wonton in the hot oil. Cook, turning once, until it is golden, about 1 minute. Adjust heat if necessary. Cook several wontons at a time, as long as they do not crowd each other.

~ Wontons are to be eaten hot. They can be kept briefly in a warm oven.

APRICOT DIPPING SAUCE

makes about 175 g/6 oz

---

*This simple sweet-sour sauce with an oriental accent goes well with fried
foods like Crab Wontons (left), Spring Rolls (page 17) or Coconut Prawns (page 96).
For an extra spicy twist, add red pepper flakes. Hoisin sauce can be
found in the oriental section of many supermarkets.*

*175 g/6 oz apricot jam or more as needed
30 ml/2 tbsp Hoisin sauce
30 ml/2 tbsp cider vinegar
1 tsp red pepper flakes, optional*

~ Put the apricot jam in a small saucepan. Heat the jam until it liquefies. Strain it into a measuring jug. If it doesn't equal 120 ml/4 fl oz, cook a little more jam. If the jam is a particularly chunky variety, it may take as much as 350 g/12 oz to yield 120 ml/4 fl oz syrup. Discard the solids.

~ Return the syrup to the saucepan. Add the remaining ingredients and cook briefly, just until the sauce is well blended. Serve warm or at room temperature.

SMOKED TROUT PÂTÉ

makes about 225 g/8 oz

Serve this easy, elegant spread with crackers or toast rounds.

225 g/8 oz smoked trout
75 g/3 oz cream cheese, softened to room temperature
2 tsp capers, drained
2 spring onions, finely chopped
15 ml/1 tbsp fresh lemon juice
½ tsp horseradish
¼ tsp pepper
15–30 ml/1–2 tbsp mayonnaise

~ Remove any skin and bones from trout. Break into chunks and put it in a mixing bowl or food processor with the remaining ingredients, except mayonnaise. Mix with a beater or processor. This spread is good either smooth or chunky. Add enough mayonnaise to thin to desired consistency. Taste and adjust seasonings. For pâté with a kick, add a little more horseradish. Refrigerate until about 20 minutes before serving.

◄ *Smoked Trout Pâté*

COLD PRAWNS WITH CHILLI-MUSTARD SAUCE

makes 6 servings

The combination of chilli and mustard in a creamy sauce is a perfect complement to cold prawns or cold crab. The prawns and sauce can be prepared hours in advance, then refrigerated. This recipe makes six appetizer servings. To increase or decrease the portions, allow about 100 g/4 oz a person. You can use any size prawns except very small ones. Reduce the amount of red pepper flakes to 1 tsp for a milder sauce.

½ onion, sliced
1 lemon, sliced
2 tbsp whole mustard seeds
1 tbsp whole coriander seeds
1 tsp whole peppercorns
2 tsp dried red pepper flakes
700 g/1½ lb prawns, shelled and deveined

SAUCE
175 ml/6 fl oz soured cream
75 ml/5 tbsp mayonnaise
3 tbsp Dijon mustard
5 ml/1 tsp Worcestershire sauce
2 tsp dried red pepper flakes

~ Fill a large pan with water. Add all the ingredients except the prawns and sauce. Bring the water to the boil, then boil for 10 minutes to develop flavour.

~ Add the prawns and let them cook just until prawns are opaque and tightly curled, about 2 minutes, depending on size. Do not overcook them or they will become tough. Drain and immediately plunge prawns into cold water to stop the cooking. Drain and refrigerate.

~ Combine all the sauce ingredients. Refrigerate for at least 2 hours to let flavours blend. Then serve with the prawns.

ROASTING CHILLIES

Some chillies have to be roasted in order to remove their coarse skin, which is difficult for some people to digest. Other chillies and ordinary red peppers are roasted to improve the flavour. Large chillies, including Anaheims and poblanos, must be roasted to remove the skin. Small chillies, including jalapeños and serranos, have edible skins and are roasted purely for flavour. Red peppers also have edible skins, but are delicious roasted.

Chillies can be roasted whole or in pieces. On a barbecue grill, they are easier to handle when roasted whole. Under a grill, they brown more evenly when cut into nearly flat pieces.

If grilling on a barbecue, place the whole chillies over glowing coals. As each section blisters and blackens, turn the chilli, until it is blistered all over.

If roasting under a grill, place the pieces skin side up on a grill-proof pan or piece of foil. Remove the pieces as they blacken and blister; they will not all be done at the same moment.

Immediately after removing the chillies from the grill, place them in a bag, covered bowl or foil pouch to steam. Let them steam about 10 minutes to loosen the skin. Then with a knife, scrape or peel off the blistered skin. It's okay if a few bits of skin remain.

Remember that chillies (but not peppers) contain capsaicin. That's the substance that makes chillies hot – and it also will make your skin burn. Protect your hands by wearing rubber gloves when cutting chillies. Alternatively, wrap a plastic bag around your hand.

ROAST JALAPEÑO CHEESE SPREAD

makes about 225 g/8 oz

Roasting the jalapeños is the secret to this bearably spicy cream cheese spread. It takes the edge off the chillies' raw heat and brings out their flavour. Serve the spread with crackers or crudités. (See notes on Roasting Chillies, left.)

3 jalapeño chillies
100 g/4 oz tomato, chopped and seeded
225 g/8 oz cream cheese, softened to room temperature
2 spring onions, finely chopped
2 tbsp chopped fresh coriander
10 ml/2 tsp fresh lime juice

~ Roast the jalapeños under a grill or on a barbecue until skins are blackened on all sides. Put the chillies in a bag or a foil pouch to steam for 10 minutes.

~ Put the chopped tomato in a colander or sieve to let the juices run while you work with the jalapeños.

~ Wearing rubber gloves to protect your fingers, scrape the charred skins off the chillies. Cut off the stalks and cut the chillies in half. Remove seeds and membranes. Finely chop the jalapeños.

~ Put the jalapeños, tomato, and remaining ingredients in a bowl, then beat with an electric mixer until well blended. Although the spread is best served at room temperature, it should be stored in the refrigerator if it is not to be used right away.

TAPENADE

makes about 225 g / 8 oz

—

*There are olive orchards the length of California's great Central Valley, where
the climate is sometimes reminiscent of the Mediterranean. Tapenade, made with olives,
anchovies, basil and sun-dried tomatoes, carries more than a whiff of the Mediterranean.
Spread tapenade on bread or crackers, use it to stuff hard-boiled eggs, or toss it with hot pasta.
If you use dried tomatoes that are not packed in oil, place them in a small heatproof bowl and
pour over just enough boiling water to cover them. Let them stand for 5 minutes,
then remove them from the water and pat them dry. If fresh basil is not available,
substitute 15 g/½ oz chopped fresh parsley and 1 tbsp dried basil.*

100 g/4 oz stoned black olives
100 g/4 oz stoned Kalamata, Niçoise or
Spanish green olives
6 anchovies
1 clove garlic
3 tbsp capers
50 g/2 oz dried tomato halves, packed in oil
about 15 g/½ oz fresh basil, chopped
1 tsp chopped fresh thyme or ¼ tsp dried
¼ tsp black pepper
10 ml/2 tsp fresh lemon juice
30–45 ml/2–3 tbsp olive oil

~ Combine all the ingredients in a blender or
food processor. Process until ingredients are well
chopped, but stop before the mixture turns into
a smooth paste. Add a little extra olive oil if
mixture is too dry.

CHILLI CON QUESO TAMALITOS

makes about 24 tamalitos

—

*Tamales are among the most delicious and the most versatile of Mexican foods.
Stuffed with spicy meat, savoury cheese or sweet fruit fillings, they can be a main dish, side dish,
snack or dessert. Tamales do require an afternoon's work, however. In many Mexican homes, the making
of a huge batch of tamales for holiday celebrations is a party in itself. These little tamales,
stuffed with cheese and roasted chillies, are delicious party food, although unwrapping the corn husks
can be a bit messy. They can be eaten plain or with Salsa (recipe follows) or enchilada sauce.
Masa, dried corn husks and fresh chillies are staples of Mexican cooking and can be
found in well-stocked supermarkets. Prepared masa dough is also available
in some stores. To serve, leave the tamales in the husks and let guests unwrap them.
(Be sure to tell them not to eat the corn husks; I have had guests unfamiliar with tamales
try to eat them.) Serve with Salsa or enchilada sauce, if desired.*

1 packet dried corn husks

DOUGH

150 g/5 oz vegetable fat
275 g/10 oz ground masa
1 tsp ground cumin
1 tsp salt
1/2 tsp baking powder
about 300 ml/1/2 pt water

FILLING

350 g/12 oz Monterey Jack or Cheddar cheese,
grated
8 jalapeño chillies, or 3 Anaheims or poblanos,
roasted, seeded, peeled and chopped (see
notes on Roasting Chillies, page 26)
1 clove garlic, crushed
40 g/1½ oz onion, finely chopped

~ Separate and soak the corn husks in warm water for 2 hours. Discard damaged ones. Drain softened husks and dry them between layers of kitchen paper towels.

~ Beat the fat until it is fluffy. Beat in the masa, cumin, salt and baking powder. Beat in the water a little at a time. Leave the dough to rest a few minutes, then beat it until it is fluffy.

~ In a separate bowl, mix the grated cheese, chopped chillies, garlic and onion. Stir so it is well blended.

~ Arrange the ingredients in an assembly line: the corn husks, masa dough, filling, and a few extra husks, torn into strips. You will need kitchen paper towels to blot the corn husks dry, a butter knife to spread the masa dough, a spoon for the cheese-chilli filling, and a bowl or plate for the assembled tamalitos.

~ The perfect corn husk for a tamalito is about 12.5 cm/5 in wide at its midpoint. Feel the husk. You will notice that one side is ribbed and the other is fairly smooth. You will be spreading the masa dough on the smooth side. Blot the smooth side dry. Pick up some masa dough with the butter knife and spread it across the middle of the corn husk. You want a strip of masa dough 7.5–10 cm/3–4 in tall, centred between the top and bottom of the husk, and spread across the entire width of the corn husk, to the very edges. It should be spread solidly but

thinly, about the thickness of cream cheese on a bagel or peanut butter on a sandwich.

~ Now take a large tablespoonful of the cheese filling and place it in the middle of the masa dough. Fold the 2 sides over, pressing on the masa at the edge of the corn husk to seal it. Pinch together the corn husk immediately above and below the masa, and tie it at either end with a strip of corn husk.

~ Continue this process until you have used all the masa and filling.

~ The tamales must be steamed. There are steamers made just for this purpose, but there are other alternatives. You can cook the tamales in a steamer insert over boiling water in a saucepan, making a tent of foil to seal in the steam if the lid won't fit. Or you can do what I do: Put about 5 cm/2 in of water in the bottom of a large saucepan. Put a steamer insert upside down in the saucepan. Use a knife to punch some holes in a disposable pie tin. Put the pie tin right side up, on top of the steamer. Put the tamales in the pie tin, leaving room for steam to circulate among them. Cover with any leftover corn husks and a clean towel to absorb excess moisture. Put the lid on the saucepan, and bring the water to the boil.

~ Steam for about 1 hour, checking after 30 to 40 minutes to be sure the water has not boiled away. Tamales are done when they are firm and the dough does not stick to the husk.

SALSA
makes about 350 ml / 12 fl oz
—

This is a basic salsa, made with grilled tomatoes for extra flavour. You can grill the tomatoes, but they won't have the same smokey flavour. The best salsas are chopped by hand, but if you prefer a soupier salsa, chop one – and only one – tomato in the food processor.

It is a moderately spicy salsa if you include 2 jalapeños and all the seeds and veins. For a hotter salsa, add another unseeded chilli – or substitute the fiery habanero chilli. To make it less spicy, remove some or all of the jalapeños' veins and seeds. This salsa is excellent not only with crisps or over Mexican food, but also with grilled meat, poultry and fish. For an unusual twist, add 2 tsp grated fresh ginger or 2 tbsp chopped fresh mint to the salsa.

3 large or 4 medium tomatoes
75 g/3 oz onion, finely chopped
2 cloves garlic, crushed
2 jalapeño chillies, finely chopped
2–3 tbsp finely chopped fresh coriander
30 ml/2 tbsp fresh lime juice
15 ml/1 tbsp olive oil
salt to taste

~ Preheat the grill or prepare coals in a barbecue. If you grill the tomatoes, you will need a grill tray that has sides to catch the tomato juice. Although less sturdy, you can substitute a double thickness of foil, with the sides pinched up to form a rim.
~ Core the tomatoes, cut them in half horizontally, and gently squeeze out the seeds. Place the tomatoes, cut side down, on the grill pan or the barbecue grill. If barbecueing, turn tomatoes over when the cut edges are partly browned, and continue grilling just long enough to loosen the skins. If grilling, grill until skins are mostly blackened and slip off easily. Remove from heat and set aside to cool. Juices will continue draining.
~ While the tomatoes are cooling, chop the remaining ingredients. Chop the cooled tomatoes and add them to the salsa. Leave to stand about 30 minutes, then taste and adjust seasonings.

*From fresh scallops and halibut to wild mushrooms
and asparagus, there are flavours, aromas and textures for
every palate, from fresh and light to hale and hearty.*

SOUPS AND STEWS

CHILLED MELON SANGRIA SOUP

makes 6 servings

Chilled fruit soup, made with melons from California's Imperial or San Joaquin Valley, is a delightful start to a summer meal. Use honeydew, cantaloupe, Crenshaw, Persian or casaba melons. The soup highlights the flavour of the melon, so be sure to pick ripe melons. You can substitute lemonade or soda water or more orange juice for the wine.

about 1 large or 2 small cantaloupe melons, cubed
120 ml/4 fl oz sweet white wine, such as
Riesling or Gewürztraminer
120 ml/4 fl oz orange juice
30 ml/2 tbsp fresh lime juice
½ tsp grated nutmeg
1 tbsp honey, optional
strawberries for garnish

~ Place all the ingredients except the honey and strawberries in blender or food processor. Process until the melon is puréed and ingredients are well mixed. Taste and add honey if needed. Chill. Serve cold, garnished with strawberries.

HALIBUT CHOWDER

makes 6 servings

Hearty fish chowders are a staple of the coastal communities of Canada and Alaska. This chowder uses the popular halibut from the waters of the northern Pacific. The sturdy halibut stands up well in chowder that is thick with corn and potatoes. The chowder gets some zip from tangy dried tomatoes.

4 rashers of bacon
1 medium onion, chopped
2 sticks celery, chopped
1 litre/1¾ pt fish stock, clam juice or chicken stock,
or a combination
1 bay leaf
¼ tsp dried thyme
½ tsp paprika
¼ tsp pepper
75 g/3 oz dried tomato halves, diced
1 medium potato, peeled and cut into
1-cm/½-in dice
175 g/6 oz sweetcorn kernels
450 g/1 lb halibut, boned, skinned and cut into
2.5-cm/1-in cubes
250 ml/8 fl oz double cream
salt to taste

~ Fry the bacon dry in a large pan. When the bacon is crisp, remove it and let it drain on kitchen paper towels. Crumble the bacon and save it for topping the soup.
~ Add the onion and celery to the bacon fat and sauté 5 minutes. Add stock, seasonings and tomatoes. Bring to the boil. Simmer 5 minutes. Add the potatoes. Simmer until potatoes are not quite tender, about 7 minutes. Add corn, halibut and cream. Cook until halibut turns snowy white, 3–4 minutes, but don't allow the chowder to boil. Taste and add salt if needed. Ladle into bowls and garnish with crumbled bacon.

Halibut Chowder ➤

COCONUT PRAWN SOUP

makes 4 servings

This delicious soup has its roots in Thailand. The stock – spicy but not hot – is flavoured by a mix of herbs widely used in South East Asia and generally available in the Americas. It is popular in Hawaii and all along the West Coast where Southeast Asian immigrants have influenced the cuisine. Fresh lemongrass is available in some well-stocked supermarkets. If it is not available, substitute 15 ml/1 tbsp fresh lemon juice and 1 tsp grated lemon rind.

15 ml/1 tbsp peanut or vegetable oil
50 g/2 oz onion, chopped
450 ml/¾ pt fish or chicken stock, or a combination
30-cm/12-inch tender inner stalk of fresh lemongrass, finely chopped
2 cloves garlic, crushed
2 tsp grated fresh ginger
1 serrano or jalapeño chilli, finely chopped
4 tbsp chopped fresh coriander
450 ml/¾ pt coconut milk
450 g/1 lb prawns, shelled and deveined
salt and pepper to taste
25 g/1 oz spring onion, chopped

~ Heat the oil in a large saucepan. Add the onion and sauté until it starts to turn golden, about 15 minutes. Add the stock, lemongrass, garlic, ginger, chilli (include the seeds if a spicier soup is desired), and 2 tbsp coriander. Lower heat and let the soup simmer for 10 minutes to develop flavours. Add coconut milk and heat to just below boiling. If using large prawns, cut into bite-size pieces. Add the prawns and continue cooking until prawns turn white and curl tightly, about 2 minutes. Taste, add salt and pepper, and adjust other seasonings if needed.
~ Serve soup garnished with spring onions and remaining 2 tbsp coriander.

◄ *Coconut Prawn Soup*

BARBECUED TOMATO SOUP

makes 4 servings

This soup, served cold, has the smokey flavour of barbecued tomatoes and sweet red peppers. The tomatoes can be grilled rather than barbecued, but they won't have the same smokey flavour. This soup portrays the taste of fresh ripe tomatoes, so don't use hard, pink ones.

2 cloves garlic, crushed
4 tbsp chopped fresh basil
¼ tsp freshly ground black pepper
45 ml/3 tbsp olive oil
1.8 kg/4 lb ripe tomatoes
2 sweet red peppers
350 ml/12 fl oz chicken stock
Tabasco sauce, to taste
½ tsp salt, or more to taste
soured cream and chives for garnish

~ Ignite the coals on a barbecue and let them burn until flames die and coals are mostly covered in white ash.
~ Combine the garlic, basil, black pepper and olive oil in a small bowl. Press the garlic with the back of a spoon to release juices. Let the oil mixture steep while you barbecue the vegetables.
~ Core the tomatoes, cut them in half horizontally and squeeze out the seeds. Cut the red peppers into sections that lie as flat as possible. Remove seeds and core. Put the tomatoes, cut side down, on the barbecue. Put the peppers, skin side down, on the barbecue. (It helps if you have a tray that goes on top of the barbecue grid and keeps small items from slipping into the coals.)

~ Cook the peppers until the skin is almost completely blackened, but don't expect them to cook evenly. Do not turn the peppers over. Remove them from the grid and put them in a bag or a foil pouch. Cook the tomatoes until the cut edges are slightly blackened. Turn them over and cook until the skins are partly blackened. Remove tomatoes and put them in a colander to drain and cool.
~ After the peppers have been sealed in the bag or foil pouch for 10 minutes, remove them and peel off the skin. It's okay if a little bit of the flesh is blackened. Dice peppers and set aside.
~ Remove the tomatoes from the colander, but use caution because the tomatoes will retain heat and could burn your fingers. Slip the skins off the tomatoes. Don't cut blackened bits off the tomato flesh. Coarsely chop the tomatoes.
~ Put the tomatoes, red pepper, garlic-oil mixture, and chicken stock in a medium saucepan. Bring soup to the boil, then reduce heat and simmer uncovered 30 minutes, stirring occasionally.
~ Taste the stock and add Tabasco sauce and salt to taste. Remove soup from heat. Leave to cool slightly. In batches, purée the soup in a blender or food processor, until you have the desired consistency. Refrigerate at least 2 hours.
~ Serve soup cold, garnished with a large spoonful of soured cream and a sprinkling of chives.

CREAM OF ASPARAGUS SOUP

makes 4 servings

This creamy asparagus soup, lightly flavoured with tarragon, is a perfect way to celebrate the arrival of spring and the season's first asparagus crop. It's light enough to be the first course of dinner, but paired with bread and salad, also makes a substantial lunch.

450 g/1 lb asparagus, fresh or frozen
750 ml/1¼ pt chicken stock
50 g/2 oz onion, chopped
1 stick celery, diced
1½ tsp fresh tarragon or ½ tsp dried
25 g/1 oz butter
2 tbsp flour
250 ml/8 fl oz double cream
⅛ tsp white pepper
salt

~ Wash the asparagus. Snap off and discard the tough ends. In a frying pan, bring 350 ml/12 fl oz water to the boil. Put half the asparagus in the water and cook until barely tender, 3–4 minutes. Remove asparagus from the water and set aside. Repeat with the second batch of asparagus. Remove the asparagus and cut off the tips. Save the water.
~ Put the cooking water, chicken stock, onion and celery in a medium saucepan. Bring to the boil, then simmer 5 minutes. Add the asparagus stalks and the tarragon, and simmer 5 minutes longer.
~ Remove the soup from the heat. In a blender or food processor, purée the soup. Return it to the pan.
~ While the soup is reheating, make a roux by melting the butter in a small pan. Add the flour. Cook, stirring constantly, until mixture is bubbling steadily. Add a spoonful of the puréed soup to the roux. It will immediately form a thick paste. Add 250 ml/8 fl oz of the puréed soup, a little at a time, stirring constantly. Pour the roux mixture in the soup and whisk until it is smooth.
~ Add cream and pepper. Heat until almost boiling. Taste and add salt if necessary. Add asparagus tips to soup, and serve.

WILD MUSHROOM SOUP

makes 4–6 servings

Dried wild mushrooms add a lovely, musky taste to this elegant soup. It can be made with ordinary mushrooms, but a mix of porcini, shitake, oyster or other mushrooms give it more interesting flavour and texture.

25 g/1 oz dried wild mushrooms
65 g/2½ oz butter
100 g/4 oz onion, chopped
450 g/1 lb mixed wild and button mushrooms, cleaned and chopped
1 litre/1¼ pt beef or chicken stock, or a combination of both
2 tbsp flour
2 tbsp chopped fresh parsley
½ tsp dried basil
⅛ tsp black pepper
60 ml/4 tbsp Madeira or vermouth
salt to taste
250 ml/8 fl oz soured cream

~ Rinse the dried mushrooms free of grit. Put them in a small bowl. Pour 250 ml/8 fl oz boiling water over them. Let them soak for 1 hour. Remove the mushrooms, saving the water. Trim off woody stalks, if necessary. Chop mushrooms. Strain the water or pour it off carefully, to remove any sand.
~ Melt 15 g/½ oz butter in heavy saucepan. Add the onions and sauté 5 minutes. Add 25 g/1 oz butter and the fresh mushrooms. Sauté 10 minutes. Add the dried mushrooms, the mushroom soaking water, and stock. Bring soup to the boil. Reduce heat and simmer 20 minutes. While the soup is simmering, melt the remaining 25 g/1 oz butter in a small pan. Add the flour and stir well to make a roux. Add a little of the hot stock to the roux. It will immediately turn into a paste. Whisk in about 120 ml/4 fl oz more of the stock, a little at a time. Then add the roux to the soup and whisk in.
~ After soup has simmered 20 minutes, add parsley, basil and pepper. Simmer 5 minutes. Add Madeira or vermouth. Taste and add salt if needed. Stir in soured cream and remove soup from heat immediately, serve.

BROCCOLI CHEESE SOUP

makes 4–5 servings

This is a West Coast alternative to the beer-cheese soups so popular in the Midwest. It uses broccoli from California and Cheddar cheese from the Oregon coastal city of Tillamook, known for its cheese. You can substitute 250 ml/8 fl oz beer for 250 ml/8 fl oz of the chicken stock.

50 g/2 oz butter
25 g/1 oz celery, finely diced
25 g/1 oz onion, finely chopped
25 g/1 oz carrot, finely chopped
1 clove garlic, crushed
2 tbsp flour
¼ tsp dry mustard
½ tsp dried basil
½ tsp dried thyme
⅛ tsp pepper
⅛ tsp cayenne
750 ml/1¼ pt chicken stock
250 ml/8 fl oz milk
175 g/6 oz broccoli, chopped
225 g/8 oz Tillamook or medium Cheddar cheese, grated
salt to taste
snipped chives for garnish

~ Melt the butter in a heavy saucepan. Add the celery, onion and carrot. Sauté 5 minutes. Add the garlic and sauté 1 minute. Add the flour, dry mustard, basil, thyme, pepper and cayenne. Stir in, making a roux. Whisk in a little chicken stock, then gradually add remaining stock and milk, whisking after each addition. Bring to the boil. Add the broccoli. Simmer until broccoli is tender, about 10 minutes. Blend in cheese. Taste and add salt if needed. Whisk until smooth and heated through, but do not allow soup to boil.
~ Garnish with snipped chives.

Broccoli Cheese Soup ➤

ALBONDIGAS SOUP

makes 6 servings

*Albondigas soup is a hearty Mexican soup of meatballs and vegetables.
With bread and a salad, it makes a meal. This is a moderately spicy soup. For a milder soup,
remove seeds and veins from the jalapeños. To peel tomatoes, cut a small x in the
skin at the base, then place in boiling water for 30–60 seconds, until skin at base starts
to curl. Remove and leave to cool for a few minutes. Skin should peel away easily.
To substitute minced chicken or turkey for the beef and pork, increase the amount
of breadcrumbs to 25 g/1 oz, and substitute chicken stock for the beef stock.*

225 g/8 oz minced beef
225 g/8 oz minced pork
1 egg, lightly beaten with fork
15 g/½ oz breadcrumbs
50 g/2 oz courgette, grated
40 g/1½ oz onion, finely chopped
½ tsp salt
⅛ tsp ground cumin
2 jalapeño chillies, stalks removed
1 large or 2 small tomatoes, peeled and cored
½ medium onion
2 cloves garlic
1 tsp dried oregano
15 g/½ oz lard or 15 ml/1 tbsp vegetable oil
1.5 litres/2½ pt beef or chicken stock,
or a combination
2 carrots, peeled and sliced
1 stick celery, trimmed and sliced
1 small courgette, sliced
2 tbsp chopped fresh coriander
salt to taste

~ Make meatballs by combining the beef, pork, egg, breadcrumbs, grated courgette, finely chopped onion, salt and cumin. Mix well and roll into walnut-sized balls. Set aside.
~ Put the jalapeños, tomato, onion, garlic and oregano in food processor and process until it make a chunky sauce.
~ Heat the lard or oil in a frying pan. Add the tomato sauce and fry until slightly thickened, 3–4 minutes.
~ Put this purée and meat stock in a large saucepan and bring to the boil. Add the meatballs. Cook 35 minutes over medium heat. Add carrots and celery. Cook 5 minutes. Add the courgette and cook 5 minutes more. Add coriander and cook 2 minutes. Add salt to taste.

SPICY SCALLOP BISQUE

makes 6 servings

*Fresh scallops from the Pacific Ocean are the
basis for this spicy bisque, thick with puréed
tomato and leek. Roasted jalapeño chillies
add spice – omit the seeds and veins if you
want only a hint of heat.*

15 g/½ oz butter
1 leek, white part only, chopped
1 carrot, chopped
1 stick celery, chopped
1 clove garlic, crushed
350 g/12 oz tomatoes, peeled, seeded and chopped
2 jalapeño chillies, roasted, peeled and chopped
(see notes on Roasting Chillies, page 26)
1 tbsp chopped fresh parsley
¼ tsp dried thyme
½ tsp dried basil
pinch of black pepper
450 ml/¾ pt clam stock
250 ml/8 fl oz dry white wine
350 g/12 oz scallops
250 ml/8 fl oz milk
250 ml/8 fl oz double cream
salt to taste

~ Melt the butter in a large, heavy pan. Add the leek, carrot and celery. Sauté for 10 minutes. Add the garlic and sauté 1 minute. Add tomatoes, jalapeños, parsley, thyme, basil, pepper, clam stock and wine. Bring the soup to the boil. Reduce heat. Simmer, stirring occasionally, for 30 minutes.
~ Add the scallops. Cook until scallops turn opaque white, 2–3 minutes. Do not overcook as scallops toughen easily. Remove from heat. Purée in blender or food processor, in small batches if necessary.
~ Return bisque to heat. Add milk and cream and heat until just below boiling. Taste and add salt if needed.

◄ *Albongdigas Soup*

SAN FRANCISCO CIOPPINO

makes 10–12 servings

If San Francisco has a signature dish, it is cioppino, a wonderful seafood stew that highlights the Pacific Ocean's Dungeness crab. Its origins are in a modest Italian fish soup, ciuppin, which in turn is a more rustic version of bouillabaisse. However, unlike the Mediterranean versions, which emphasize fish, cioppino emphasizes shellfish, especially crab. A typical cioppino is likely to include crab, prawns, mussels, clams, sometimes lobster or scallops, and a little fish, maybe swordfish or sea bass. The stock is a rich, garlicky tomato stock, usually flavoured with wine. To the north, in Washington's Puget Sound region, cooks make a regional variation of cioppino, which showcases salmon alongside the Dungeness crab. Cioppino is a dramatic dish for a dinner party, served simply with green salad and crusty sourdough bread, another San Francisco speciality. Best of all, the stock can be prepared a day in advance, then reheated at dinner time, with the seafood added at the last minute. Cioppino is usually served in large, wide bowls. Be sure to provide tools for cracking crab shells, dishes for guests to discard shells, and finger bowls or lots of napkins.

*120 ml/4 fl oz plus 30 ml/2 tbsp olive oil
1 large onion, chopped
3 leeks, white part only, chopped
1 red pepper, chopped
1 green pepper, chopped
8 cloves garlic, crushed
700 g/1½ lb fresh tomatoes, peeled, seeded and chopped, or 3 x 425-g/15-oz. cans of whole tomatoes, chopped
4 tbsp chopped fresh parsley
2 tsp dried basil
1 tsp dried oregano
½ tsp dried thyme
2 bay leaves
¼ tsp dried red pepper flakes, or more to taste
450 ml/¾ pt dry red wine, such as pinot noir
2 litres/3½ pt fish stock, bought or homemade (recipe follows)
salt to taste
2 large Dungeness crabs, cooked, cracked and cleaned
2 dozen clams in their shells, scrubbed
2 dozen mussels in their shells, scrubbed
450 g/1 lb sea bass, swordfish or other sturdy, non-oily fish, cut into 2.5 cm/1-in cubes
700 g/1½ lb prawns, shelled and deveined*

~ In a very large saucepan (my largest stockpot is barely big enough, once the crabs are added), heat 120 ml/4 fl oz oil. Add the onion, leeks and peppers. Sauté 10 minutes.

~ In the meantime, heat the remaining 30 ml/ 2 tbsp olive oil in a very small sauté pan. Add the garlic and sauté 2 minutes. If the garlic starts browning too fast, remove the pan from the heat. The residual heat in the oil will continue cooking the garlic. Add the garlic and oil to the saucepan. (It may be my imagination, but I think this brings out the garlic flavour better. Otherwise, it seems the garlic is stewed in the juices of the other vegetables and the flavour never develops as well.)

~ Add to the saucepan the tomatoes, herbs, pepper flakes, wine and fish stock. Bring soup to the boil, then reduce heat and leave to simmer, uncovered, 45 minutes. Taste, add more red pepper flakes if a spicier stock is desired, and add salt if needed. If you are making the stock in advance, remove it from the heat, cool and refrigerate. About 30 minutes before serving time, return it to the cooker and bring it to the boil.

~ Add seafood in this order: first, the crab, about 15 minutes before serving time. Add the mussels or clams about 5 minutes later. Add the fish 7–8 minutes before serving time, and finally, about 3 minutes before eating, add the prawns.

~ Remove and discard the bay leaves, as well as any mussels or clams whose shells did not open. Put some seafood in each bowl, making sure everyone gets a selection, then ladle stock over it.

FISH STOCK

Some supermarkets make their own fish stock, which they sell frozen. Ask whether the stock is at normal strength, or is concentrated and needs to be diluted. If the shop does not carry stock, ask your fishmonger for about 1.5 kg/ 3 lb of fish bones, heads and tails, from non-oily fish. Make sure the gills are removed, and that the fish parts are washed clean of any blood, and rinse under cold running water for several minutes.

*30 ml/2 tbsp olive oil
2 onions, sliced
2 carrots, chopped
3 sticks celery, chopped
6–8 parsley sprigs
2 bay leaves
fish parts*

~ Heat the oil in a saucepan. Add the onions, carrots and celery. Sauté 10 minutes. Add the parsley, bay leaves and fish parts, and enough water to cover by 2.5 cm/1 in. Bring to the boil. Reduce heat and simmer, uncovered, 25 minutes. Occasionally skim off any scum. Pour stock through a strainer and discard solids. Taste stock. If it tastes weak, return it to the heat and simmer 10–15 minutes longer.

VEGETARIAN LENTIL STEW

makes 8 servings

This spicy stew of lentils, rice and vegetables is not spicy-hot; rather it is a melange of flavours. For extra richness, the onions are sautéed slowly until they are golden brown, and the red peppers are roasted.

25 g/1 oz tbsp butter
2 onions, sliced
2 red peppers
15 ml/1 tbsp olive oil
4 cloves garlic, crushed
½ tsp ground cumin
1 tsp dried basil
½ tsp dried oregano
½ tsp dried thyme
1 tsp chilli powder
¼ tsp cayenne
450 ml/¾ pt vegetable stock
225 g/8 oz dried lentils, picked over
120 ml/4 fl oz dry red wine
225 g/8 oz tomato sauce
225–275 g/8–10 oz cooked white rice
2 medium tomatoes, peeled, seeded
and chopped
salt to taste
50 g/2 oz spring onions, chopped
soured cream for serving

~ Melt the butter in a large frying pan. Add the onions and sauté over low heat until they are golden brown, 20–25 minutes.

~ Preheat the grill. Cut each red pepper into 3 or 4 relatively flat pieces. Place skin side up on a pan under the grill. Cook until skins are blistered and blackened. Remove peppers from grill and place in a bag or a foil pouch. Let the peppers steam for 10 minutes, then remove them and peel off the skin. Dice the peppers.

~ Heat the olive oil in a large pan. Add the garlic and sauté 1 minute. Add spices and sauté 1 minute longer. Do not let the spices scorch. If the oil is too hot, take it off the burner. The spices will continue to cook.

~ Carefully add the vegetable stock and 750 ml/ 1¼ pt of water to the garlic-spice mix. Add the lentils, wine and tomato sauce. Bring to the boil and let the lentils simmer until they are tender, 15–30 minutes, depending on how they were processed. Add the rice and tomatoes. Simmer 5 minutes. Taste and adjust salt and other seasonings. Add the spring onions. Ladle into bowls and top with a dollop of soured cream.

CHILLI COLORADO

makes 6 servings

*Chilli Colorado – or Red Chilli Stew – is a very basic beef or pork stew.
It began as a way of cooking very tough meat, no beans or tomatoes, and somehow evolved
into the popular chilli con carne that bears little resemblance to the original dish. The main
ingredients are dried chillies and cubed meat that are simmered in beef stock for several hours.
There's no point in making Chilli Colorado if you don't like spicy food, but you can vary the
heat by using different chillies. California chillies are mild, ancho chillies (dried poblanos) are
moderately hot, and New Mexico chillies are very hot. Chilli Colorado is wonderful
rolled up in warm corn tortillas, or it can be served over plain white rice.*

6 dried New Mexico, ancho or California
chillies, or a combination
30 ml/2 tbsp vegetable oil
1 onion, chopped
2 cloves garlic, crushed
1 kg/2 lb pork or beef stew meat, cut into
2.5 cm/1-inch cubes
1 litre/1¼ pt beef stock
1 tsp ground cumin
1 tsp dried oregano
salt to taste

~ Preheat the oven to 120°C/250°F/Gas Mark ½.
Put the chillies on a baking sheet. Roast them
until they darken and become crisp and produce a
toasty smell. Do not let them burn or the bitter
taste will ruin the stew. Put the chillies in a small
saucepan. Cover them with water. (If necessary,
weigh down the chillies with a small bowl – they
may bob above the water otherwise.) Simmer
chillies for 20 minutes or so to soften. Remove
the stalks, then purée the chillies and cooking
water in a blender or food processor. Strain the
purée to remove seeds and bits of skin. If desired,
purée the bits that remain in the strainer with a
small amount of water, in order to get the last bit
of flavour from the chillies. Discard the strained
solids.

~ In a large, heavy saucepan, heat 15 ml/1 tbsp
oil. Add the onion and sauté 5 minutes. Add the
garlic and sauté 1 minute more. Remove the
onions and garlic with a slotted spoon and set
aside. Add the remaining 15 ml/1 tbsp oil if
needed. Add beef or pork and cook until lightly
browned on all sides.

~ Add stock to the pan. Return onions and
garlic, add chilli purée, cumin and oregano.
Bring stew to the boil. Reduce heat and leave
stew to simmer, uncovered, at least 2 hours,
until meat is falling apart. Sauce should reduce
and thicken, but you may need to add a little
stock or water during the cooking. Add salt to
taste and serve.

Stunningly beautiful summer delights feature in this selection of tasty salads; scallops and crab, artichokes, papayas and pears. The colours are vibrant and the flavours fresh.

SALADS

POACHED SCALLOPS WITH BASIL VINAIGRETTE

makes 4 servings

*This lovely salad features cold poached scallops that have been marinated in a
garlicky basil vinaigrette. You can substitute other cooked seafood such as prawns, mussels
or squid, or a combination. Ripe tomatoes always make a perfect match with basil.
For the greens, try round lettuce or a mixture of baby greens.*

450 g/1 lb scallops
250 ml/8 fl oz dry white wine
½ lemon, sliced
½ small onion, cut into wedges
1 tbsp coarsely chopped fresh basil or 1 tsp dried
about 100 g/4 oz salad greens
2 ripe tomatoes, cored and cut into wedges

BASIL VINAIGRETTE
4 tbsp fresh basil leaves
2 cloves garlic
120 ml/4 fl oz olive oil
30 ml/2 tbsp white wine vinegar
15 ml/1 tbsp fresh lemon juice
¼ tsp salt
pinch of black pepper

~ Rinse the scallops. If you are using large
scallops, cut them into quarters.

~ In a medium saucepan, combine the wine,
250 ml/8 fl oz water, lemon slices, onion and
basil. Bring the poaching liquids to the boil,
then reduce heat and simmer for 5 minutes to
develop flavour.

~ Add the scallops. Cover the pan and simmer
2 minutes. Then remove pan from heat, leave
cover on pan, and leave scallops to stand in the
poaching liquid 10 minutes. Drain the scallops
and let them cool.

~ Make the basil vinaigrette by blending the
ingredients in a blender or food processor. Put
the scallops in a non-reactive bowl. Pour the
vinaigrette over the scallops. Stir the scallops so
all sides are coated with dressing. Leave them to
marinate in the refrigerator 30 minutes–
2 hours before using.

~ Divide salad greens and tomato wedges
among 4 salad plates. Remove the scallops from
the vinaigrette and put on top of the lettuce.
Dress the salads with a little of the vinaigrette.

SALAD NIÇOISE WITH FRESH GRILLED TUNA

makes 4 servings

*This traditional salad takes on a whole new character when it is
topped with a warm grilled tuna steak instead of canned tuna.
If you like your tuna rare, cut the steaks a little thicker.*

450 g/1 lb new potatoes
350 g/12 oz green beans, as thin as possible
1 small head Cos lettuce, washed,
dried and torn into bite-size pieces
2 hard-boiled eggs, sliced
2 ripe tomatoes, cut into wedges
16–20 Niçoise olives
8–12 anchovy fillets
30 ml/2 tbsp olive oil
30 ml/2 tbsp fresh lime juice
4 tuna steaks, 1 cm/½-inch thick
(about 100 g/4 oz each)
salt and pepper
Tarragon Vinaigrette (page 51)

~ Ignite the coals in the barbecue and allow them
to flame while you are preparing ingredients. Oil
the grill so tuna does not stick.

~ Scrub the new potatoes and, if desired, peel
them. Put them in a pan of boiling water.
Cook until tender, 15–20 minutes. Drain.

~ Trim green beans and put them in a pan of
boiling water. Boil until tender-crisp, 5–10
minutes, depending on their size and age. Drain
and plunge into cold water. Drain again.

~ Arrange lettuce on 4 plates. Divide potatoes and
green beans among them. Top with sliced eggs,
tomatoes, olives and anchovies.

~ Mix the olive oil and lime juice. Brush it over
both sides of the tuna steaks. Season the steaks
with salt and pepper. When barbecue flames have
died and coals are glowing, place the tuna on the
oiled grill. Cook, turning once, about
3 minutes a side, until tuna is cooked through but
is still juicy. Remove tuna from grill and place a
steak on top of each salad. Dress with vinaigrette
and serve warm.

WARM ARTICHOKE SALAD

makes 4 servings

In this unusual but delicious salad, warm artichoke hearts are mixed with roasted red peppers, almonds and feta cheese, then topped with the Tarragon Vinaigrette on page 51.

4 jumbo artichokes or 6 large
1 lemon, halved
1 clove garlic, peeled and crushed
15 ml/1 tbsp olive oil
1 red pepper
25 g/1 oz flaked almonds
75 g/3 oz feta cheese
about 50 ml/2 fl oz Tarragon Vinaigrette (page 51)

~ Holding each artichoke by the stalk, break off the leaves by pulling each backward and down, letting it snap off from the base. Leave the choke and the most tender inner leaves intact for now. Cut off the stalk. Rub the cut surface of the artichoke with the cut surface of a lemon half to keep the artichoke from turning brown.
~ In a saucepan or other large pan, bring water to boil. Add the crushed garlic clove and the olive oil, and squeeze the juice from the remaining lemon half. Add the trimmed artichoke hearts to the boiling water. Cook until the hearts are tender but still firm. This will be 20–30 minutes, depending on the size and age of the artichokes.

~ While the artichokes are cooking, roast the red pepper. Preheat the grill. Cut pepper into quarters and remove seeds and ribs. Put the pepper quarters skin side up on a grill pan about 7.5 cm/3 in below grill. Grill until skins are blistered and mostly blackened. Remove from the oven and put pepper in a bag to steam for 10 minutes.
~ Reset oven to 150°C/300°F/Gas Mark 2. When the grill is no longer giving off heat, spread the almonds on a small baking sheet and toast them until they are lightly browned, 8–10 minutes. Monitor the almonds closely, as they can burn suddenly. Remove almonds and set them aside to cool.
~ Peel the skins from the red pepper and dice the pepper.
~ When the artichokes are tender, remove them from the water and leave them to stand for a few minutes to let them cool slightly. Pull off the rest of the leaves, and scoop out the choke with a spoon.
~ Slice the artichoke hearts and mix with the almonds and diced pepper. Crumble the feta cheese over the salad and top with Tarragon Vinaigrette. Serve warm.

PEAR GORGONZOLA SALAD

makes 4 servings

This composed salad features the complementary match of pears and Gorgonzola cheese. Use whatever type of pear is in season.

1 head Cos lettuce, washed, separated and trimmed
2 pears
2 avocados
about 50 g/2 oz Gorgonzola cheese, crumbled
25 g/1 oz flaked almonds
vinaigrette of your choice

~ Divide the lettuce leaves between 6 plates. Cut unpeeled pears into thin lengthways wedges, and core. Peel avocados and cut into thin lengthways wedges. Alternate pear and avocado slices in sunburst arrangement on each plate. Sprinkle cheese and almonds over salad. Serve with vinaigrette on the side.

Pear Gorgonzola Salad ➤

CRAB SALAD WITH AVOCADO AND PAPAYA

makes 4 servings

—

This cool summer salad mixes avocados and pistachios from California, papaya from Hawaii, and crab from the waters of the Pacific Ocean. It is topped with a creamy dressing.

DRESSING

75 g/3 oz mayonnaise
2 tsp Dijon mustard
7.5 ml/1½ tsp fresh lemon juice
50 ml/2 fl oz double cream
⅛ tsp salt
⅛ tsp white pepper

SALAD

8 large lettuce leaves, preferably round or red leaf lettuce
1 large papaya
1 large avocado
450 g/1 lb cooked crabmeat
2 tbsp roasted pistachio nuts, coarsely chopped
2 spring onions, chopped

~ Whisk together the mayonnaise, mustard and lemon juice. Whip the cream until soft peaks form. Fold it into the mayonnaise mixture. Stir in salt and pepper. The dressing will improve if it stands in the refrigerator for several hours while the flavours blend.

~ Clean and dry the lettuce leaves and arrange them on 4 plates. Cut the papaya and avocado into thin wedges and peel. Arrange them on the salad plates. Divide crabmeat among the salads. Put dressing on salads, and top with pistachios and spring onions.

◄ *Crab Salad with Avocado and Papaya*

GRILLED BEEF SALAD

makes 4 servings

—

This salad is a delicious way to use up leftover London Grill (page 74). You may find yourself grilling steak for the sole purpose of having leftovers for this salad. Serve it with Tarragon Vinaigrette (recipe follows) or your favourite vinaigrette, or with a thick Roquefort dressing.

1 small head Cos lettuce, washed, dried and torn into bite-size pieces
450 g/1 lb cold grilled beef, thinly sliced
2 large, ripe tomatoes, cut into wedges
2 thin slices of onion, separated into rings
½ red pepper, seeded and cut into thin strips
1 large avocado, diced
dressing of your choice

~ Divide lettuce among 4 plates. Top with beef, tomatoes, onion, pepper and avocado. Serve with dressing of your choice.

TARRAGON VINAIGRETTE

makes about 250 ml/8 fl oz

—

The addition of an egg yolk makes this a slightly richer and thicker vinaigrette.

1 egg yolk
30 ml/2 tbsp white wine vinegar
15 ml/1 tbsp fresh lemon juice
150 ml/¼ pt olive oil
pinch of freshly ground pepper
pinch of salt, if desired
2 tbsp fresh tarragon or 2 tsp dried

~ Combine all the ingredients in a blender or food processor.

MESCLUN SALAD

makes 4 servings

Mesclun is a mixture of salad greens, usually young, wild lettuces and greens like arugula, radicchio, lamb's lettuce and watercress. Mesclun mixtures are increasingly available in supermarkets, but they are a particular delight picked fresh from the garden. If you mix your own, be aware that some lettuces and greens are bitter and should be used sparingly. This salad is a simple one, adding only walnuts, goats' cheese and mushrooms to the greens, so be sure the greens are absolutely fresh and crisp. Leave time for the mushrooms to marinate. Marinate the mushrooms and dress the salad with the Tarragon Vinaigrette on page 51, or use another of your choosing.

120 ml/4 fl oz vinaigrette
100 g/4 oz mushrooms, sliced
about 100 g/4 oz mixed greens, torn into
bite-size pieces
50 g/2 oz goats' cheese
50 g/2 oz walnut pieces

~ Pour the vinaigrette over the sliced mushrooms and leave them to marinate in the refrigerator for at least 1 hour.
~ Divide the salad greens among 4 plates. Just before serving, spoon some of the mushrooms and vinaigrette over the greens. Crumble the goats' cheese and scatter the walnuts over the salads. Dress the salads with additional vinaigrette, if desired.

JICAMA SALAD

makes 6 servings

Jicama, a crisp, white-fleshed tuber with a mild flavour, is eaten in Mexico with lime juice and chilli powder. Here it adds a delightful crunch to an unusual salad.

1 medium jicama (about 450 g/1 lb)
1 mango
2 oranges
½ red or sweet onion
½ red pepper

DRESSING
50 ml/2 fl oz vegetable oil
30 ml/2 tbsp dry red wine
30 ml/2 tbsp honey
30 ml/2 tbsp orange juice

~ Peel the jicama and cut it into julienne strips. Peel and dice the mango. Peel the oranges, separate into sections, and cut away the membranes. Thinly slice the onion, then separate the rings. Seed and cut the pepper into julienne strips. Combine all ingredients in salad bowl. Combine all the dressing ingredients and stir or shake until well blended. Toss salad with the dressing.

BLACK BEAN PAPAYA SALAD

makes 4 servings

Black Bean Papaya Salad, a marriage of Mexican, Hawaiian and oriental ingredients, gets its heat from fresh ginger and jalapeño chilli, and its sweetness from papaya. It is an excellent side dish with grilled meat and fish. Use canned black beans if necessary, but the flavour and texture are better if you start with dried beans and simmer them until tender. If lemongrass is not available, substitute 1 tbsp grated lemon rind.

350 g/12 oz black beans, cooked
1 papaya, peeled, seeded and diced
1 jalapeño chilli, unseeded, finely chopped
40 g/1½ oz onion, chopped
40 g/1½ oz red pepper, chopped
2 tsp finely grated fresh ginger
2 tbsp chopped fresh mint
1 tbsp chopped fresh basil
1 stalk lemongrass, tender inner stalk only,
finely chopped
50 ml/2 fl oz fresh lime juice
15 ml/1 tbsp olive oil
salt and pepper to taste

~ Combine all the ingredients. Leave them to stand 20 minutes at room temperature, then taste and adjust seasonings. Refrigerate until ready to eat.

Black Bean Papaya Salad ➤

MUSSELS VINAIGRETTE WITH SWEET ONION AND HAZELNUTS

makes 4 servings

This salad celebrates the food of the Pacific Northwest with mussels from the ocean, sweet onions from Washington, hazelnuts from the orchards, and spinach from the cool valleys. The mussels should be prepared early in the day. If you clean the spinach and toast the hazelnuts at the same time, the salads can be assembled at the last minute.

20–24 small mussels
250 ml/8 fl oz dry white wine
75 ml/5 tbsp red wine vinegar
1 clove garlic, crushed
2 tsp Dijon mustard
150 ml/¼ pt olive oil
¼ tsp salt
⅛ tsp pepper
2 tbsp chopped fresh parsley
225 g/8 oz young spinach leaves, trimmed, washed, dried and torn into bite-size pieces
4 slices of sweet onion, separated into rings
40 g/1½ oz toasted hazelnuts, coarsely chopped

~ Scrub the mussels with a brush to remove grit. Remove beards. Discard any mussels that do not close. Put mussels in a pan. Add wine and 250 ml/ 8 fl oz water. Bring to the boil, cover and reduce heat. Cook 5–7 minutes until mussels open. Discard any that did not open. Put the mussels in a shallow, non-reactive dish.

~ While the mussels are cooking, make the vinaigrette. Combine red wine vinegar, garlic, mustard, olive oil, salt, pepper and parsley. Whisk or shake until well blended. Pour over the hot mussels. Cover and refrigerate mussels at least 6 hours, occasionally spooning marinade over mussels.

~ About 30 minutes before serving time, remove the mussels from refrigerator and let them come to room temperature. Divide the spinach between 4 plates. Top with onion rings and hazelnuts. Divide the mussels among the plates. Spoon vinaigrette marinade over the salads.

LENTIL-HAZELNUT SALAD

makes 4–6 servings

Virtually all of the lentils grown in the United States come from the Palouse region of the Pacific Northwest – an area that sprawls through eastern Oregon and Washington and parts of Idaho and Montana. Although they are a dried bean, lentils require no soaking. Any type of lentil may be used in this recipe. However, cooking times may vary, so consult the cooking instructions on the packet. Here, they are mixed with hazelnuts, chopped vegetables and vinaigrette for a salad that tastes good cold and even better warm. Serve it as a salad, or a base for grilled fish. To roast hazelnuts, spread them on a small baking sheet. Place them in a 180°C/350°F/Gas Mark 4 oven. Roast until they start to brown, about 10 minutes, but watch them closely as they can go quickly from roasted to scorched.

225 g/8 oz lentils, picked over for stones
1 tsp salt
225 g/8 oz fresh asparagus
40 g/1½ oz roasted chopped hazelnuts
50 g/2 oz spring onions, chopped
1 red pepper, seeded and diced
1 tbsp chopped fresh basil or 1 tsp dried
30 ml/2 tbsp red wine vinegar
60 ml/4 tbsp olive oil
1 tsp Dijon mustard
1 clove garlic, crushed
¼ tsp black pepper
few drops Tabasco sauce

~ Place the lentils in a medium saucepan with the salt and 750 ml/1¼ pt water. Bring water to the boil. Cook until tender, 15–30 minutes depending on type. Drain.

~ While the lentils are cooking, prepare the asparagus. Snap off tough ends and cut stalks into 2.5-cm/1-in pieces. Bring a pan of water to the boil. Cook asparagus until tender crisp, about 3 minutes. Drain.

~ Mix the lentils, asparagus, hazelnuts, spring onions, red pepper and basil, if using fresh basil. Combine vinegar, oil, mustard, garlic, black pepper and dried basil, if using. Whisk or shake until well blended. Pour over the lentil salad, then toss salad to blend. Taste and add Tabasco sauce.

Simple recipes, delicious results. Coriander, rosemary, mint and
thyme are just a few of the aromatic fresh herbs used to enhance and
bring out the true flavours of the coastline's abundant produce.

VEGETABLES AND RICE

ASPARAGUS WITH SALSA VINAIGRETTE

makes 4 servings

For a healthy alternative to butter or a heavy sauce, top steamed asparagus with a salsa vinaigrette. It can be served hot or cold.

450 g/1 lb fresh asparagus, washed and trimmed
120 ml/4 fl oz Salsa (page 29), or your favourite salsa
75 ml/5 tbsp olive oil
15 ml/1 tbsp red wine vinegar

~ Steam the asparagus over boiling water until the spears are tender, 10–12 minutes.

~ While the asparagus is cooking, combine the salsa, oil and vinegar in a blender or food processor.
~ Remove the asparagus from heat and put in a serving dish. Pour vinaigrette over asparagus. Serve hot, or leave the asparagus to marinate in the vinaigrette and serve it cold.

TAHITIAN RICE

makes 4 servings

The addition of mango, ginger and nutmeg give this rice dish an exotic flavour. Serve it with roasted chicken or grilled fish. You can substitute flaked almonds if macadamia nuts are not available.

450 ml/¾ pt chicken stock
7 g/¼ oz butter
¼ tsp ground ginger
¼ tsp grated nutmeg
200 g/7 oz white rice
1 mango, peeled and diced
50 g/2 oz macadamia nuts, chopped
40 g/1½ oz celery, chopped
50 g/2 oz spring onions, chopped

~ Bring the chicken stock, butter, ginger and nutmeg to the boil in a small saucepan. Stir in the rice. Cover and reduce heat. Cook until rice is tender and stock is absorbed, about 20 minutes.
~ Preheat the oven to 180°C/350°F/Gas Mark 4. Lightly butter a casserole dish.
~ Place the rice into a large bowl. Stir in the mango, nuts, celery and onion. Spoon into the casserole dish. Bake rice, covered, for 30 minutes.

Tahitian Rice ➤

FRIED SWEET POTATOES

makes 6 servings

Ginger and cayenne give sweet potatoes a spicy kick. This side dish goes particularly well with pork or poultry.

3 large sweet potatoes
50 g/2 oz brown sugar
½ tsp ground ginger
¼ tsp cayenne
75 g/3 oz butter

~ Peel the sweet potatoes and cut them into 1 cm/½-in thick slices. Fill a large saucepan three-quarters full with water and bring water to the boil. Add the potato slices and boil until they are barely tender, 8–10 minutes. Drain potatoes.
~ Mix the sugar, ginger and cayenne in a small bowl and set aside.
~ Melt the butter in a large frying pan. Add the potatoes and sauté for 1 minute. Sprinkle the sugar mixture over the potatoes and sauté for 1 minute longer. Serve hot.

◄ *Fried Sweet Potatoes*

CALIFORNIA WILD RICE STUFFING

makes 10–14 servings

Wild rice, the seed of wild grasses once thought to grow only in and around Minnesota, is now cultivated successfully by California farmers. Wild rice and almonds from the Sacramento Valley, raisins from near Fresno, and lemons from around Visalia make this truly a California dish.

250 g/9 oz wild rice
1 tsp salt
25 g/1 oz butter
25 g/1 oz onion, chopped
225 g/8 oz mushrooms, coarsely chopped
75 g/3 oz flaked almonds, toasted
75 g/6 oz sultanas
2 tsp grated lemon rind
250 ml/8 fl oz soured cream
3 tbsp chopped fresh parsley
3 spring onions, chopped
½ tsp black pepper
extra salt, if needed

~ Rinse and drain the wild rice to remove any grit. Put in a large saucepan. Add teaspoon of salt and 1.5 litres/2½ pt water. Bring water to the boil. Reduce heat and simmer, uncovered, adding water if needed, until grains burst. This usually takes 45 minutes–1 hour, but you should start checking after about 35 minutes. When nearly all of the grains have burst, drain rice.
~ While the rice is cooking, melt the butter in a frying pan. Sauté onions for 5 minutes. Add mushrooms and sauté until they start exuding moisture, about 6 minutes.
~ In a large bowl, combine cooked rice, mushroom mixture, almonds, raisins, lemon rind, soured cream, parsley, spring onions and pepper. Taste and add salt if needed.
~ Stuff bird or fish, or place stuffing in lightly buttered casserole dish. Cover and bake for 20 minutes at 180°C/350°F/Gas Mark 4.

ROAST VEGETABLES

makes 6–8 servings

One of the simplest ways to prepare vegetables is to roast them. Roasting works particularly well with sturdy vegetables, such as carrots, potatoes and turnips. Vegetables like tomatoes that have a high water content do not turn out as well. If possible, let the herbs steep in the olive oil for a day before using.

2 medium onions, peeled and quartered
2 red peppers, seeded and quartered
450 g/1 lb green beans, trimmed
450 g/1 lb carrots, peeled and cut into 7.5 cm/3-in pieces
about 45 ml/3 tbsp olive oil
1 tsp dried thyme or rosemary

~ Preheat the oven to 200°C/400°F/Gas Mark 6. If possible, use a wide, shallow ovenproof dish that is attractive enough to serve from. Arrange the vegetables in the baking dish. The carrots should not be more than 2 layers deep, the onions only one layer. Drizzle olive oil and herbs over the vegetables. Turn vegetables so all sides are coated. Leaving pan uncovered, roast the vegetables until they are tender, 30 to 40 minutes. During roasting, baste vegetables with the olive oil.

BAKED FENNEL

makes 4 servings

Florence fennel, or finocchio, is a root vegetable with a pleasant anise flavour. Here it is boiled first in chicken stock, then baked with Parmesan cheese for an Italian-style dish.

1 large or 2 small fennel bulbs (about 700 g/1½ lb)
750 ml/1¼ pt chicken stock
salt and pepper
25 g/1 oz butter
25 g/1 oz Parmesan cheese, freshly grated

~ Preheat the oven to 180°C/350°F/Gas Mark 4. Butter a medium casserole dish.

~ Trim off the fennel stalks and discard. Cut the bulb into wedges. Bring the chicken stock to the boil in a medium saucepan. Add the fennel and boil until the fennel is barely tender, about 12 minutes. Drain the fennel. Arrange it in the casserole dish. Season with salt and pepper. Dot with butter and sprinkle with Parmesan cheese. Bake about 10 minutes, until the cheese is melted.

GRILLED PORTOBELLO MUSHROOMS

makes 4 servings

Big and meaty, portobello mushrooms are perfect for grilling, either whole or thickly sliced. We've included directions for a homemade marinade, but as a shortcut, you can use a bottled vinaigrette. It's easy to soak them in marinade early in the day, then put them on the grill when you're barbecuing meat or fish.

8 large portobello mushrooms
75 ml/5 tbsp olive oil
15 ml/1 tbsp balsamic vinegar
10 ml/2 tsp fresh lemon juice
2 cloves garlic, put through a garlic press
½ tsp salt
¼ tsp pepper
1 tbsp chopped fresh basil or tarragon

~ Clean the mushrooms and lay them in a shallow, non-reactive dish. Combine the remaining ingredients and stir or shake well. Pour dressing over mushrooms. Let them marinate in the refrigerator for 2–24 hours.
~ Place the mushrooms on barbecue over glowing coals. Cook whole mushrooms 3–4 minutes a side. For sliced mushrooms, if you don't have a grid for grilling small items, use a sheet of foil with holes punched in it. Grill slices 2–3 minutes a side.
~ Serve hot.

Grilled Portobello Mushrooms ➤

HERB-ROASTED POTATOES

makes 4 servings

These crispy potatoes make a flavourful alternative to fried potatoes.

50 ml/2 fl oz olive oil
2 tbsp dried onion flakes
2 cloves garlic, crushed
½ tsp dried rosemary
450 g/1 lb potatoes
2 tbsp chopped fresh parsley
1 tsp paprika
½ tsp salt
¼ tsp pepper

~ Preheat the oven to 230°C/450°F/Gas Mark 8. Have ready a baking sheet or large, shallow baking tin.
~ Mix the oil, onion, garlic and rosemary and set aside to let flavours develop. (This is even better if mixed earlier in the day.)
~ Do not peel the potatoes. Cut them into wedges. Put oil mixture, parsley, paprika, salt and pepper in large plastic bag. Add the potatoes. Close the bag and shake until potatoes are well coated.
~ Place the potatoes onto the baking sheet or tin and drizzle the oil mixture over them. Bake, stirring occasionally, until potatoes are golden and cooked through, about 30 minutes, depending on the thickness of the wedges.

MANGETOUT AND CARROTS IN MINT-BASIL BUTTER

makes 4 servings

Tender spring carrots and mangetout make a tasty side dish when they are tossed with Thai-inspired mint-basil butter. Use fresh herbs if they are available.

350 g/12 oz carrots, peeled and sliced
100 g/4 oz mangetout, trimmed
40 g/1½ oz butter
2 tbsp chopped fresh basil or 2 tsp dried
2 tbsp chopped fresh mint or 2 tsp dried
salt and pepper to taste

~ Steam the carrots over boiling water until not quite tender, about 8 minutes. Add the mangetout and steam until tender, about 3 minutes.
~ Melt the butter in small sauté pan. Add the herbs and cook over low heat a minute or so to develop flavour. Put the vegetables in a serving dish and toss with herbed butter. Season with salt and pepper, if desired.

BAKED POTATO CASSEROLE

makes 4 servings

Here's a hearty dish made of sliced potatoes, tossed with garlic and chives, then topped with crumbled bacon and Cheddar cheese. Reduced-fat cheese makes a less oily dish.

3 large potatoes, peeled and
cut into 5-mm/¼-in slices
30 ml/2 tbsp olive oil
2 cloves garlic, crushed
1 tsp salt
¼ tsp black pepper
2 tbsp snipped fresh chives
4 rashers of bacon, cooked and crumbled
100 g/4 oz Cheddar cheese, grated

~ Preheat the oven to 230°C/450°F/Gas Mark 8.
~ Toss the sliced potatoes with olive oil, garlic, salt, pepper and 1 tbsp chives. Put the potatoes in an ungreased casserole dish. Bake 20 minutes, uncovered. Remove from oven. Sprinkle with the remaining 1 tbsp chives, bacon and cheese. Put back in the oven and cook until potatoes are tender, 10–15 minutes.

BROCCOLI WITH WALNUTS AND RED PEPPER

makes 4 servings

*Walnuts and roasted red pepper dress up ordinary steamed broccoli.
I like to include part of the broccoli stalk, thinly sliced.*

450 g/1 lb broccoli, including stalks, cut up
30 ml/2 tbsp olive oil
40 g/1½ oz walnuts, coarsely chopped
1 tbsp chopped fresh basil or 1 tsp dried
5 ml/1 tsp fresh lemon juice
1 roasted red pepper, peeled and diced
(See notes on Roasting Chillies, page 26)
100 g/4 oz feta cheese, crumbled

~ Steam the broccoli until almost cooked to desired tenderness.
~ Heat the oil in a large frying pan. Add the walnuts and sauté 1 minute over medium heat. Add basil and sauté 30 seconds. Add the broccoli and sauté 2 minutes.
~ Remove the broccoli from heat. Spoon broccoli and walnuts into a serving dish. Add lemon juice and red pepper. Toss. Add feta cheese and serve.

ARTICHOKES WITH CHIPOTLE DIPPING SAUCE

makes 4 servings

Here's a sauce that will give artichokes quite a kick: mayonnaise flavoured with a smoked jalapeño chilli. Serve it as a first course at dinner, or instead of a more traditional vegetable.

SAUCE
250 ml/8 fl oz mayonnaise
30 ml/2 tbsp extra-virgin olive oil
1 canned chipotle chilli, finely chopped
2 tbsp chopped fresh coriander

ARTICHOKES
15 ml/1 tbsp fresh lemon juice
15 ml/1 tbsp olive oil
1 clove garlic, crushed
4 large artichokes

~ Whisk together the sauce ingredients and leave to stand, refrigerated, for several hours to let flavours develop fully.

~ Fill a large pan with water. Add the lemon juice, olive oil and garlic clove. Bring the water to the boil.

~ While the water is heating, prepare the artichokes. Trim off all but 2.5 cm/1 in of stalk. With a sharp, heavy knife, cut off the leaf tips. When the water has come to the boil, put the artichokes in the water. Cook until artichokes are tender, about 40–50 minutes. Remove from water, turn artichokes upside down, and drain well. Serve with sauce.

STIR-FRIED ASPARAGUS

makes 4–6 servings

Sweet red pepper and water chestnuts add colour and crunch in this low-fat asparagus dish.

700 g/1½ lb fresh asparagus
15 ml/1 tbsp vegetable oil
5 ml/1 tsp sesame oil
50 g/2 oz red pepper, diced
50 g/2 oz water chestnuts, sliced
10–15 ml/2–3 tsp rice wine vinegar, optional

~ Trim the asparagus and cut it diagonally into 5-cm/2-in pieces. Cook the asparagus in boiling water about 2 minutes for slender stalks, 3 minutes for fat stalks. Remove and plunge into cold water. Drain well.

~ Heat both oils in a wok, and swirl the wok so that the oil coats the lower sides. Add the asparagus and stir-fry 2 minutes. Add the red pepper and stir-fry 1 minute. Add the water chestnuts and stir-fry 1 minute. Serve asparagus hot, with a splash of rice wine vinegar if desired.

Stir-Fried Asparagus ➤

BAKED MEXICAN RICE

makes 6 servings

Corn, chillies, cheese and soured cream make this a substantial side dish that could also serve as a vegetarian main dish. It goes particularly well with grilled fish or chicken. It's an easy dish to make. The only complicated step is roasting and peeling the chillies (see notes on Roasting Chillies, page 26). If you're short of time, simply substitute canned chopped chillies, but the flavour of freshly roasted jalapeños is superior.

450 g/1 lb cooked white rice
2 jalapeño chillies, roasted, peeled, seeded and chopped
175 g/6 oz sweetcorn kernels
250 ml/8 fl oz soured cream
100 g/4 oz Cheddar cheese, grated
2 tbsp chopped fresh coriander
2 tbsp chopped fresh parsley
40 g/1½ oz spring onions, chopped

~ Preheat the oven to 180°C/350°F/Gas Mark 4.
~ Combine all the ingredients. Put the mixture in an ungreased casserole dish. Bake, uncovered, for 30 minutes.

◄ Baked Mexican Rice

SAUTEED SPINACH ALOHA

makes 6 servings

Ginger, garlic, soy sauce and macadamia nuts give spinach a whole new character in this easy dish.

1 kg/2 lb fresh spinach, thoroughly washed and trimmed
45 ml/3 tbsp vegetable oil
25 g/1 oz macadamia nuts, chopped
2 tsp grated fresh ginger
2 cloves garlic, crushed
30 ml/2 tbsp soy sauce
5–10ml/1–2 tsp rice wine vinegar

~ Bring water to the boil in a large pan. Have ready a large bowl of iced water. Blanch spinach for 1 minute in the boiling water, then quickly remove it and plunge it into the bowl of iced water. This quick process preserves the bright green of the spinach and keeps it from overcooking. Drain the spinach well, then squeeze out as much moisture as possible. Transfer the spinach to a cutting board and coarsely chop it.
~ Heat the oil in a large frying pan. Add the macadamia nuts. Sauté the nuts until they just begin to brown, about 1 minute. Add the ginger and garlic. Sauté about 30 seconds longer. Do not allow the garlic to brown. Add the spinach and soy sauce, and sauté 2–3 minutes longer, until the spinach is heated through. Remove from heat, splash with rice vinegar, and serve immediately.

VEGETARIAN BLACK BEANS WITH GOATS' CHEESE

makes 4–6 servings

*Black beans are seasoned with chipotle chillies, smoked jalapeño chillies that
add heat and a wonderful flavour. Goats' cheese provides a cool but pungent contrast
to the spicy mixture. Serve the beans in bowls with the cheese crumbled over the top, or
wrapped in warm corn tortillas smeared with goats' cheese.*

*400 g/14 oz dried black beans, picked over for stones
700 g/1½ lb tomatoes, chopped
1 large onion, chopped
3 cloves garlic, crushed
2 chipotle chillies, either canned or dried
2–3 tsp salt
5 tbsp chopped fresh coriander
75 g/3 oz spring onions, chopped
½ tsp dried oregano
1 tsp ground cumin
175 g/6 oz goats' cheese*

~ Put the beans in large pan with 1.75 litres/ 3 pt water. Soak overnight. Or bring beans and water to the boil for 2 minutes, then cover pan, turn off heat and stand for 1 hour. Drain beans and rinse. Rinse the pan. Put the beans back in the pan and barely cover them with fresh water. Watch the water level while the beans are cooking and add water if necessary, but avoid having to pour off excess water. Add 225 g/8 oz chopped tomatoes, onion and garlic. Bring to the boil, then reduce heat and simmer beans uncovered until they are tender, about 1 hour 15 minutes.

~ If you are using canned chipotles, remove the stalks. Finely chop chillies and add them to the beans. If you are using dried chillies, wait until the beans have cooked 45 minutes. Then put the chillies in a small bowl and pour 150 ml/ ¼ pt boiling water over them. Let them steep until they are pliable, about 30 minutes, but check occasionally to be sure they are covered with water. Remove the stalks, cut the chillies crossways into strips, then make a few lengthways cuts. Put the chillies and the soaking water into a food processor or blender. Add about 100 g/4 oz of the beans. (The chillies

don't have enough bulk by themselves to be chopped fine by most food processors.) Purée the mixture, then add it to the bean pan.

~ Pour any excess water off from the beans. Add 2 tsp salt and lightly mash them – some beans should remain whole. Mix in remaining tomatoes, coriander, spring onions, oregano and cumin. Taste and add more salt if necessary.

~ Ladle the beans into bowls and crumble goats' cheese over the top. Or smear warm corn tortillas with goats' cheese, add beans and roll up.

POLENTA WITH WILD MUSHROOMS

makes 4 servings

A rich variety of edible wild mushrooms grows in Oregon and Washington, including porcini, oyster, chanterelle and morel mushrooms. Here, they are sautéed with leeks and ordinary mushrooms, then served over hot polenta. Polenta should be cooked long and slowly to develop its flavour. Much of the polenta available in supermarkets is instant polenta, which calls for only about 5 minutes of cooking. Even the quick-cook polentas benefit from 5–10 minutes additional cooking time.

POLENTA
1 tbsp salt
175 g/6 oz polenta
50 g/2 oz butter, cut into pieces

MUSHROOMS
1 kg/2 lb mixed wild and button mushrooms
40 g/1½ oz butter
30 ml/2 tbsp olive oil
75 g/3 oz leek, white part only, chopped
3 cloves garlic, crushed
120 ml/4 fl oz dry white wine
½ tsp dried thyme
½ tsp pepper
½ tsp salt or to taste
3 tbsp chopped fresh parsley

~ Bring the salt and 750 ml/1¼ pt of water to the boil in a pan. Pour the polenta into the boiling water in a thin stream, stirring constantly so it does not form lumps. Cook, stirring constantly, until polenta becomes very thick and pulls away from the side of the pan. If it is an instant polenta, continue cooking and stirring for 5–10 minutes. When it is done, stir in the butter, piece by piece, until it is well blended. Pour into 1 large or 4 individual serving dishes. The polenta can be kept warm in the oven while the mushrooms are cooking, if necessary, or set aside until needed for serving.
~ Clean and trim the mushrooms. If you are using shitake mushrooms, cut off the woody stalks. Slice the mushrooms.
~ Heat the butter and olive oil in a large frying pan. Add the leeks and sauté for 5 minutes. Add the garlic and sauté 1 minute. Add mushrooms and sauté until most moisture has evaporated. Add the wine and cook over a high heat for 2 minutes to reduce the wine. Add thyme, pepper and salt. Taste and adjust seasonings. Stir in parsley. Cook for 2 minutes, then serve over the warm polenta.

Despite the wealth of seafood, meat, cheese and egg dishes are vast and
varied among the regional cuisines of the Pacific Rim, including
recipes influenced by Chinese and South East Asian tradition as well
as favourites from Alaska and Mexico.

MEAT, CHEESE
AND EGGS

LONDON GRILL

makes 6 servings

In the South, barbecue means meat that is smoke-cooked for hours and served with a top-secret sauce. On the West Coast, barbecuing means grilling – fast-cooking over glowing coals. London Grill is the quintessential West Coast barbecue. It's easy and half the work is done in advance. Here it's marinated in a garlicky red wine mixture. While the meat is cooking, grill corn on the cob or potato slices brushed with olive oil. Then serve it with salad and bread. London Grill is made from flank steak, although any steak of your choice can be used for this recipe.

175 ml/6 fl oz dry red wine
50 ml/2 fl oz olive oil
1 tbsp Dijon mustard
6 cloves garlic, crushed
1 tsp dried oregano
1 tsp dried rosemary
½ tsp black pepper
1 kg/2 lb. flank steak

~ Combine all the ingredients, except the steak, stirring or shaking until well blended. Put the steak in a sturdy, sealable plastic bag and pour the marinade over it. Leave the meat to marinate, refrigerated, 4–24 hours.
~ Prepare the coals for the barbecue. Drain the meat and discard the marinade. When the flames have died and coals are glowing, put meat on the grill directly over coals. Grill, turning once, until cooked to desired doneness. Time will depend on the heat from the coals, the thickness and cut of meat, but will probably be 7–15 minutes a side.
~ Remove meat from the grill. Leave to stand 10 minutes or so, then cut against the grain into thin slices.

PESTO CHICKEN LINGUINE

makes 6 servings

This dish turns traditional basil pesto, chicken and cream sauce into a flavourful pasta meal. The pesto and chicken can be made up to a day in advance, then refrigerated until 15 minutes before dinner. You can use boneless or bone-in chicken breasts. Decrease cooking time for boneless breasts by about 10 minutes.

25 g/1 oz walnuts
2 cloves garlic
about 25 g/1 oz fresh basil leaves
100 g/4 oz Parmesan cheese, freshly grated
120 ml/4 fl oz olive oil
½ tsp salt
pinch of freshly ground black pepper
4–6 skinless chicken breasts
450 g/1 lb linguine or other noodles
75 g/3 oz butter
450 ml/¾ pt double cream
½ tsp salt
75 g/3 oz Parmesan cheese, freshly grated
plus extra for garnish

~ Preheat the oven to 180°C/350°F/Gas Mark 4. Lightly oil a baking tin.
~ Make the pesto by putting walnuts, garlic, basil, 100 g/4 oz Parmesan, olive oil, ½ tsp salt and pepper in a food processor. Process the mixture until it is coarsely textured, but not a smooth paste.

~ Set aside 120 ml/4 fl oz of pesto. Spread the remaining pesto over the chicken breasts. Put the chicken in the baking tin. Bake until the chicken is cooked and juices run clear, 45–50 minutes. The chicken can be made ahead to this point and then cooled and refrigerated.
~ Cut or tear the cooked chicken into strips, taking care to remove any small bones. If any pesto crust flakes off, put it in the bowl with the shredded chicken.
~ Bring a large pan of salted water to the boil and add the linguine. Cook according to directions on packet. Drain.
~ Five minutes before the linguine is done, melt the butter in a large frying pan. Add the remaining pesto and cook 1 minute. Add cream, ½ tsp salt and shredded chicken. Cook 3 minutes. Stir in 75 g/3 oz Parmesan. If the frying pan is large enough, mix in the linguine. Otherwise, return the linguine to its dry cooking pan and add the sauce to the noodles. Toss until linguine is evenly coated with sauce. Serve with additional Parmesan on the side.

Pesto Chicken Linguine ➤

CARNITAS

makes 4–6 servings

Carnitas are a Mexican dish made of large chunks of pork that are stewed, then baked. The cooked meat is shredded and served with tortillas and salsa. It is a flavourful dish but not as hot as many Mexican dishes. If you use a lean cut of pork or trim away most of the fat, it will be a fairly healthy dish. Serve the shredded pork with warm corn tortillas and one or more salsas, such as Salsa (page 29) and Smokey Avocado Salsa (page 100).

1 tsp salt
2 tsp ground cumin
2 tsp mild chilli powder
2 tsp dried oregano
2 tsp garlic powder
2 tsp onion powder
¹/₂ tsp cayenne
1 kg/2 lb boneless pork, cut into 6–8 chunks
30 ml/2 tbsp vegetable oil
1 onion, quartered
2 cloves garlic, crushed

~ Combine the salt and spices in a bowl. Rub the spice mix into all sides of the meat. Leave to stand for 1 hour and absorb the spices.
~ Heat the oil in a large pan, preferably an ovenproof pan. Brown the meat in the oil, turning until lightly browned on all sides but not cooked through. Add onion, garlic and enough water to cover the meat. Bring water to the boil, reduce heat and simmer, covered, 1¹/₂ hours.
~ Preheat oven to 180°C/350°F/Gas Mark 4. Drain all but about 120 ml/4 fl oz stock. (Discard the stock or save it for making soup.) If the pan is ovenproof, put the pork and the reserved 120 ml/4 fl oz stock in the oven. Or transfer meat and stock to a baking tin. Bake for 45 minutes. Remove from the oven and leave to cool slightly. Shred meat with a fork.

◄ *Carnitas*

GRILLED PORK SKEWERS

makes 6 main-dish servings or
10–12 appetizer servings

Here's a way to eat pork that cuts down on the fat. A lean cut of pork is cubed, marinated in a lime-garlic-coriander mixture, and grilled over hot coals. Serve it with Ginger-mango Salsa (page 92). It can be used as a main dish or a hot appetizer.

1 kg/2 lb boneless loin of pork, trimmed of fat
175 ml/6 fl oz fresh lime juice
50 ml/2 fl oz olive oil
3 cloves garlic, peeled and crushed
2 tbsp chopped fresh coriander
¹/₄ tsp black pepper

~ Cut the pork into 4-cm/1¹/₂-in cubes.
~ Make the marinade by combining remaining ingredients. Put the pork in a non-reactive bowl or a plastic food storage bag. Pour the marinade over the pork. Stir pork so cubes are coated. Marinate overnight.
~ If using wooden skewers, soak 12 of them in water for 30 minutes to prevent burning them. Light barbecue coals. Drain pork and discard marinade. Divide pork into 12 portions and thread the cubes on the skewers.
~ When the barbecue flames have died and coals are glowing, place the skewers on the grill over the coals. Cook, turning once, until the pork is cooked through, 3–5 minutes a side.

GRILLED HERB-MUSTARD POUSSINS

makes 4 servings

—

Mustard and herbs flavour the marinade and the sauce that give grilled birds their delicious flavour. While you're using the barbecue, grill some very large mushrooms (page 62) to serve with the chicken.

4 poussins
175 ml/6 fl oz olive oil
50 ml/2 fl oz white wine vinegar
3 tbsp Dijon mustard
2 cloves garlic, crushed
2 tsp fresh rosemary or 1 tsp dried
1 tbsp fresh thyme or 1 tsp dried
1 tbsp fresh oregano or 1 tsp dried

MUSTARD-HERB SAUCE

about 50 g/2 oz Dijon mustard
30 ml/2 tbsp olive oil
22.5 ml/1½ tbsp fresh lemon juice
1 tsp fresh rosemary or ½ tsp dried
1½ tsp fresh thyme or ½ tsp dried
1½ tsp fresh oregano or ½ tsp dried

~ Cut the birds in half along the backbone and remove backbone. Combine remaining ingredients except those for the mustard-herb sauce. Put birds in a shallow non-reactive dish. Pour marinade over birds so they are evenly coated. Marinate in the refrigerator 2–24 hours.
~ Prepare the coals in the barbecue and ignite them. When the flames have died and coals are glowing, place the birds – spread flat like a butterfly – over the coals. Cook, turning once, until birds are browned and juices run clear when thickest part of flesh is pierced, about 20 minutes a side.
~ Combine all the ingredients for the mustard-herb sauce and about 5 minutes before the birds are done, brush both sides with the sauce.

TEA-SMOKED DUCK

makes enough meal for 4–6 salads or sandwiches

—

Tea-smoking is a popular Chinese method of flavouring duck before it is roasted. With a large wok, it's easy. Chicken, poussins and turkey breasts can be cooked the same way. Be sure the tea is fresh – like herbs, old tea loses its flavour.

2 tsp sesame seeds
1 duck (1.5–2 kg/3–4 lb)
2 tsp salt
1 tsp pepper
2 tsp grated orange rind
several wedges of unpeeled orange
2 spring onions, cut in half
about 25 g/1 oz black or jasmine tea leaves
50 g/2 oz brown sugar
65 g/2½ oz uncooked rice
3 cinnamon sticks, broken in half

~ Put the sesame seeds in a small sauté pan over medium heat. Toast the seeds, shaking occasionally to keep them from scorching, until they start to brown, 2–3 minutes. Set seeds aside to cool.
~ Remove the giblets from the duck and trim off excess fat.
~ Combine cooled sesame seeds, salt, pepper and orange rind. Rub over outside of duck. Put orange wedges and spring onions inside duck.
~ Line a large wok with heavy duty foil. Combine tea leaves, brown sugar and rice, and put in bottom of wok with cinnamon sticks. Place a rack in the wok so it sits at least 2.5 cm/ 1 in above the tea mixture, but low enough that the lid will fit snugly. Place duck on rack. Turn on high heat under wok. Leave uncovered until mixture smokes, then cover and reduce heat to medium high. Let it smoke for 20 minutes. It is very important that you do not remove lid even for a quick peek during smoking. Turn off heat, but do not remove the lid for another 20 minutes. When time is up, remove the duck. Discard the tea mixture.
~ Preheat the oven to 190°C/375°F/Gas Mark 5. Place the duck, breast side down, on a rack in a roasting tin. When the duck has been in the oven for 15 minutes, prick the skin all over with a fork to let fat run out. Repeat this step after a further 15 minutes. Roast the duck for a total of 45–60 minutes, until the juices run just slightly rosy when the thick part of thigh is pierced. Remove duck, turn over, and increase oven temperature to 230°C/450°F/Gas Mark 8. Carefully pour off and discard all but a small amount of the grease that has accumulated in the roasting tin. Return the duck to the hot oven and roast about 5 minutes longer, until duck skin is crisp but not burned. (Skip this last step for chicken or turkey.)
~ When the duck is cool enough to handle, cut meat from bones and shred.
~ To use meat in a salad, begin with mixed greens, including a few bitter greens such as endive or chicory. Add duck meat, onion, grapefruit sections, avocado wedges and a basic vinaigrette.
~ For sandwiches, serve shredded meat with small, soft, brown rolls and fresh coriander, shredded spring onions and hoisin sauce.

Tea-smoked Duck ➤

ROAST DUCK WITH APPLES

makes 2–3 servings
—

Wild duck is a favourite in Alaska, where hunting is taken seriously. But most of us have to be satisfied with domestic duck, which must be cooked in a completely different manner. Wild ducks are lean. Domestic ducks have a thick layer of fat under the skin and must be cooked so that the fat is rendered. Steaming the bird gets rid of some of the fat because it goes in the roasting tin. A 2–2.5 kg/4–5 lb domestic duck serves 2–3 people. For a sweeter gravy, substitute cherries for the apples. You can still use the apple juice as a base for the gravy, or substitute cherry juice.

1 duck (2–2.5 kg/4–5 lb)
½ lemon
salt
fresh or dried thyme, optional
1 stick celery, cut into 5-cm/2-in pieces
1 onion, peeled and halved
75 ml/5 tbsp apple juice
30 ml/2 tbsp fresh lemon juice
3 tbsp sugar
¼ tsp allspice
¼ tsp cinnamon
¼ tsp dried thyme
¼ tsp black pepper
about ½ tsp salt
2 small apples, peeled, cored and sliced
2 tbsp cornflour

~ Remove the neck and giblets from the duck, and save. Pull off loose fat and discard. Cut off wingtips and save. Rinse the bird, then wipe it dry. Rub inside and out with the cut edge of the lemon half. Rub inside and out with salt and, if desired, fresh or dried thyme.

~ Put the duck on a rack in a flameproof roasting tin. (If you don't have a flameproof roasting tin, improvise. Place a rigid steamer insert upside down in a saucepan large enough to hold the duck.) Put 2.5 cm/1 in of water in the tin with the celery and half of the onion, cut into wedges. (If you are using an upended steamer insert, place the onion and celery under the insert.) Put the tin on top of the cooker. Bring water to the boil, cover tightly, reduce heat. Let it steam for 30 minutes.

~ Preheat the oven to 170°C/325°F/Gas Mark 3.

~ Remove the duck from the tin. Remove onions and celery and set aside. Pour cooking liquids into a saucepan and set aside. Put duck on rack in roasting tin (you can also use a 23 x 33-cm/9 x 13-in cake tin). Place remaining onion half in chest cavity. Roast the duck in the oven until juices run barely rosy for medium rare, clear yellow for medium (45 minutes–75 minutes, depending on size of the duck). Do not allow it to overcook.

~ While the duck is roasting, skim the fat off the cooking liquids and discard fat. Put the neck, giblets and wingtips in a small saucepan with the degreased juices and the cooked onion and celery. Add a little water, if necessary, so duck parts are covered. Bring water to the boil. Reduce heat and simmer, uncovered. If too much water evaporates, add a little more.

~ About 10 minutes before duck is done, strain the duck stock, mashing vegetables and duck parts to get juices out. Discard the solids. You will need 175 ml/6 fl oz of stock. If you have more, cook it over high heat to reduce liquids and concentrate the flavours.

~ In a separate small saucepan, make a syrup of the apple juice, lemon juice, sugar, allspice, cinnamon, thyme, pepper and salt. Bring syrup to the boil. Add the apples. Simmer fruit in syrup 5 minutes or until the apples are tender. Remove the fruit.

~ Add the duck stock to the syrup. In a small cup, combine the cornflour with 30 ml/2 tbsp cold water and mix well. Whisk in a little of the stock, then add the cornflour mixture to the stock to make gravy. Heat until the gravy has slightly thickened.

~ Cut the duck into serving pieces. Arrange on a platter. Pour the gravy over the duck and arrange apple slices around the duck.

QUATTRO FORMAGGI PIZZA WITH PESTO

makes 4–6 servings

To some people, pizza just isn't pizza without tomato sauce and pepperoni or sausage. But California cooks were among those pioneering what is often called gourmet pizza – pizzas made with imaginative ingredients like goats' cheese or smoked salmon that just don't go with the standard tomato sauce. Here is a pizza made with pesto and four cheeses. It is delicious as it is, but can also serve as a base for your own creativity. Try it with chopped sun-dried tomatoes, or with Grilled Portobello Mushrooms (page 62).

DOUGH

7 g/¼ oz sachet dried yeast
1 tsp sugar
175 ml/6 fl oz water at 40–45°C/105°–115°F
275 g/10 oz flour
1 tsp salt
45 ml/3 tbsp olive oil, plus extra for bowl
cornmeal

FILLING

about 50 g/2 oz fresh basil leaves
40 g/1½ oz pine nuts or walnuts
75 ml/5 tbsp olive oil
5 cloves garlic
½ tsp salt
275 g/10 oz mozzarella cheese, grated
175 g/6 oz provolone cheese, grated
225 g/8 oz ricotta cheese
100 g/4 oz Parmesan cheese, freshly grated

~ Put the yeast and sugar in the warm water. Leave to stand until the yeast becomes foamy, 5–10 minutes.
~ While the yeast is proofing, mix the flour and salt in a large bowl. Add the olive oil and the yeast mixture. Stir until liquids are mostly incorporated, then begin kneading. The dough should be kneaded on a lightly floured surface for about 10 minutes.
~ Lightly oil the inside of a medium bowl. Put the dough in the bowl, then turn it over so it is coated with oil on all sides. Put a teatowel over the dough and put it in a warm place to rise.
~ While the dough is rising, make the pesto. Put the basil, nuts, olive oil, garlic and salt in a food processor. Process until it forms a rough-textured mix, but is not quite a paste.
~ Mix the cheeses in a bowl. Add the pesto to the cheese and mix well.
~ When the dough has doubled in size, about 1 hour, knock it back and divide it in half. Preheat the oven to 250°C/500°F/Gas Mark 9.
~ Roll out half the dough on a lightly floured surface until it forms a circle about 36 cm/14 in in diameter (or an oval to fit your baking sheet). Sprinkle cornmeal on a baking sheet or pizza stone. Move the dough to the baking sheet or pizza stone (it may be easier to move the dough if you fold it in quarters). Spread half the cheese-pesto mixture on the pizza, leaving a 2.5-cm/1-in edge.
~ Put the pizza on the lowest shelf of the oven. Cook until the edges turn golden brown and the cheese is bubbling, about 10 minutes. While it is baking, prepare the second pizza in the same way.

VEGETARIAN HUEVOS RANCHEROS

makes 4 servings

A traditional Mexican dish, this has become a comfort food in the American west, ranking alongside meat loaf or mashed potatoes and gravy. Many recipes call for Huevos Rancheros to be served with beans on the side, but we've incorporated the beans into this version.

175 g/6 oz black beans or canned refried beans
vegetable oil for frying
4 corn tortillas
225 g/8 oz Cheddar cheese, grated
8 eggs
about 300 ml/½ pt Salsa (page 29)
avocado slices for garnish
sliced black olives for garnish

~ Preheat the oven to 180°C/350°F/Gas Mark 4. Lightly oil 2 baking sheets. Heat the beans.
~ Heat about 5 mm/¼ in oil in a frying pan. When the oil is hot, briefly fry the tortillas one at a time. Cook just enough to heat and soften them, turning once, about 5 seconds a side. Drain on kitchen paper towels. Spread a quarter of the beans over each tortilla. Sprinkle 40 g/1½ oz cheese over each tortilla. Put the tortillas on baking sheets and put them in the oven to melt the cheese. If the cheese melts before the eggs are ready, turn the oven off but leave the tortillas in the oven with the door closed.
~ Discard all but 15 ml/1 tbsp oil from the frying pan and reheat the pan. Break 2 eggs onto a saucer, then slide eggs into hot pan. If the pan is big enough, fry 2 pairs at a time. Cook 2–3 minutes until the yolks are set, covering the pan or spooning hot oil over the yolks to cook them. If desired, turn the eggs and cook about 30 seconds longer. Repeat until all eggs are fried.
~ Put 2 eggs on each tortilla. Top with salsa and re-maining cheese. Garnish with avocados and olives.

Vegetarian Huevos Rancheros ➤

POBLANO-ROASTED CHICKEN

makes 3–4 servings
—

Moderately spicy poblano chillies with garlic, onion and spices make a tasty coating for roasted chicken. If you cannot find poblanos, substitute two Anaheim chillies and one jalapeño.

3 cloves garlic, unpeeled
15 ml/1 tbsp olive oil, or more as needed
2 poblano chillies
25 g/1 oz onion, chopped
about 2 tbsp chopped fresh coriander
1 tsp dried oregano
½ tsp ground cumin
¼ tsp salt
10 ml/2 tsp fresh lemon juice
1 oven-ready chicken (1.5–2 kg/3–4 lb), cleaned

~ Preheat the oven to 180°C/350°F/Gas Mark 4.
~ Put the garlic cloves on a piece of foil. Pour about 15 ml/1 tbsp olive oil over the garlic, enough to coat the cloves. Pull up the sides of the foil and fold over the top to form a closed pouch. Roast the garlic until soft, about 45 minutes. When they are cool enough to handle, peel the cloves.
~ Preheat the grill.
~ Cut the chillies in half lengthways. Remove seeds and stalks. Place the chillies, cut side down, on a grill pan. Grilll the chillies until skins blister and turn mostly black. Remove the chillies from the grill and place them in a bag or make a pouch of foil. Let the chillies steam in the closed bag or pouch for 10 minutes to loosen their skins. Peel off the skins.
~ Put the garlic, chillies, and remaining ingredients, except chicken, in a blender or food processor. Process until ingredients form a lumpy paste. If ingredients are too dry to form a paste, add a little olive oil.
~ Rub a little salt on the inside of the chicken. Loosen but do not remove the skin of the chicken. Cut some slits in the flesh and in the skin. Rub paste all over the outside of the chicken, pushing some into slits and under the skin. Chicken can be cooked immediately, but it is better if it stands for several hours in the refrigerator to develop flavours.
~ Preheat the oven to 190°C/375°F/Gas Mark 5. Place the chicken on a rack in a roasting tin. Roast chicken, basting occasionally with pan juices, until its juices run clear when the thick part of the thigh is pierced with a fork, about 1 hour–1 hour 20 minutes.

ORIENTAL TURKEY BREAST

makes 4–6 servings
—

Roast turkey breast, basted with a soy-orange sauce, makes an excellent excuse to eat turkey any time of year. If the basting sauce is made in advance, little work is required at dinner time. This sauce is also good on roast chicken.

30 ml/2 tbsp vegetable oil
30 ml/2 tbsp soy sauce
30 ml/2 tbsp orange juice
5 ml/1 tsp honey
1 clove garlic, peeled and put through garlic press
½ tsp dry mustard
1 turkey breast, bone in (about 1.5 kg/3 lb)

~ Preheat the oven to 180°C/350°F/Gas Mark 4. Have ready a roasting tin with rack.
~ Combine all the ingredients except the turkey. Put turkey on a rack in a roasting tin. Spoon some of the sauce over the turkey. Roast, uncovered, basting frequently with remaining sauce, about 20 minutes per 0.5 kg/1 lb.

Oriental Turkey Breast ➤

The fruits of the Pacific are abundant, from the warm waters off
Mexico to the frigid waters of Alaska. Among the various seasonings are lime
juice, sun-dried tomatoes, basil vinaigrette and macadamia nuts.

SEAFOOD

SMOKED SALMON PASTA

makes 4 servings

This rich pasta sauce features chunks of smoked salmon and shreds of prosciutto in cream.

*40 g/1½ oz butter
225–275 g/8–10 oz smoked salmon broken into 1-cm/½-in pieces
50 g/2 oz prosciutto, diced or shredded
175 ml/6 fl oz double cream
¼ tsp white pepper
1 tbsp snipped chives
about 50 g/2 oz Parmesan cheese, freshly grated
450 g/1 lb linguine or fettucine, cooked and well drained*

~ Melt the butter in a frying pan. Add the salmon and prosciutto. Cook for a minute or two, enough to heat the meat and flavour the butter. Over a low heat, stir in the cream, pepper and chives. Cook for a few minutes until the sauce thickens slightly. Stir in the Parmesan cheese so that the sauce thickens a little more. Mix sauce with noodles and serve immediately.

MAHI MAHI IN A MACADAMIA CRUST

makes 4 servings

Mahi mahi, also known as dolphin fish, is a frequent catch off the Hawaiian Islands and in other tropical waters. Here it is marinated in lime and ginger, then teamed with another Hawaiian treat, macadamia nuts. You can substitute other white fish, such as sole. Serve this with Ginger-fruit Butter (recipe follows).

*4 mahi mahi or sole fillets
(100–175 g/4–6 oz each)
75 ml/5 tbsp fresh lime juice
30 ml/2 tbsp olive oil
2 tsp finely grated fresh ginger
100 g/4 oz macadamia nuts
25 g/1 oz flour
pinch of salt and pepper
1 egg
30 ml/2 tbsp milk*

~ Put the fish in a non-reactive dish. Combine the lime juice, olive oil and ginger root and pour over fish. Let fish marinate 30–60 minutes in the refrigerator, turning the fillets once or twice to be sure they are completely coated.
~ Preheat the oven to 250°C/500°F/Gas Mark 9. Lightly oil a baking sheet or shallow pan big enough to hold all the fillets.
~ While the fish is marinating, finely grind the macadamia nuts in the food processor until they resemble coarse cornmeal. Do not over-grind or they will turn into nut butter.
~ Pour the ground nuts into a shallow bowl. Mix flour, salt and pepper in another shallow bowl. In a third bowl, beat egg and milk together with a fork.

~ Remove the fish from the marinade and drain, but leave a few bits of ginger clinging to the fish. Dip each fillet in the flour and shake off excess. Dip in egg-milk mixture, then roll fillets in nuts until they are evenly coated.
~ Place the fillets on the baking sheet or pan. Bake until the fish is opaque but still juicy, 6–8 minutes, depending on the thickness of the fillets.

GINGER-FRUIT BUTTER
makes about 175 g/6 oz

This butter is excellent with fish and baked or grilled chicken. Make it in advance, roll into a log, then slice off pats of butter as needed.

*100 g/4 oz butter, softened to room temperature
50 g/2 oz puréed mango, papaya, peach or nectarine
15 ml/1 tbsp fresh lime juice
2 tsp grated fresh ginger
1 tsp snipped fresh chives*

~ Mash the butter with a fork. Beat in the other ingredients. Roll mixture into a log and wrap in foil. Refrigerate until ready to use.

Mahi Mahi in a Macadamia Crust ➤

BAKED STUFFED SALMON

makes 10–14 servings

Long before white settlers reached the West Coast, the Indians of the Pacific Northwest caught and roasted Columbia River salmon as a staple of their diets. Strips of salmon meat were woven with slender branches, often alder wood, and roasted next to a smouldering fire. Oven-roasting salmon on hot alder or cedar planking will give the fish some of that same lovely flavour. In this recipe, baked stuffed salmon makes a dramatic main course for a dinner party. You can use California Wild Rice Stuffing (page 61).

*1 large whole salmon (3–4 kg/6–8 lb),
cleaned and scaled
salt and pepper
about 1 kg/2 lb stuffing of your choice
melted butter or olive oil*

~ Preheat the oven to 190°C/375°F/Gas Mark 5. Grease a shallow baking dish or baking sheet with sides, large enough to hold the salmon.
~ Rinse the salmon inside and out. Lightly season inside and out with salt and pepper. Stuff with stuffing, lightly packed. Place the remaining stuffing in a lightly buttered casserole dish and bake as directed in stuffing recipe. Pin edges of fish together with skewers or cocktail sticks, or sew closed with heavy thread. Brush outside of fish with melted butter or olive oil.
~ Measure the thickness of the salmon, including stuffing, at thickest point. Baking time will be approximately 10 minutes per 2.5 cm/1 in of thickness. Place in oven. Baste at least once with butter or oil while it is cooking. Salmon is done when the flesh has lost its bright red colour. There may be a bit of translucence at the thickest point, since a large fish such as this will continue to cook after it is removed from the oven.
~ Open fish and cut pieces from top or bottom. Serve with some of the stuffing from the fish. Serve casserole dish of remaining stuffing on the side.

◄ *Baked Stuffed Salmon*

FETA PRAWNS ON FUSILLI

makes 4 servings

Feta cheese and Greek olives give this dish a Mediterranean flavour. It is deceptively fast. Just have all your ingredients ready to go before you start cooking. Time the pasta so it finishes cooking just before the prawns.

*450 g/1 lb fusilli or other pasta
30 ml/2 tbsp olive oil
2 cloves garlic, crushed
15 g/½ oz butter
1 tbsp chopped fresh basil or 1 tsp dried
½ tsp fresh thyme or ¼ tsp dried
450 g/1 lb tomatoes, chopped
450 g/1 lb prawns, shelled and deveined
50 ml/2 fl oz dry white wine
¼ tsp pepper
175 g/6 oz feta cheese, crumbled
16 Greek olives
2 tsp snipped chives for garnish*

~ Cook the pasta in lots of boiling water to which you've added salt and a splash of olive oil.
~ While the pasta is cooking, make the sauce. Heat the olive oil in a large frying pan. Add the garlic and sauté 1 minute. Add butter, basil and thyme, and cook 1 minute. Add the chopped tomatoes and cook 2 minutes. Add prawns and sauté until prawns barely turn pink and are not quite cooked through, 1–2 minutes. Add wine and pepper, and cook 1 minute. Add feta cheese and olives. Remove from heat. Ladle over pasta and sprinkle with chives.

GRILLED SALMON WITH BLACK BEAN SALSA

makes 6 servings

Salmon from the waters of the northern Pacific and a Mexican black bean salsa are a wonderful combination, but the salsa will go well with just about any grilled fish. Black beans are always better if you start with the dried beans and simmer them yourself, but this recipe uses canned black beans as a shortcut.

75 ml/5 tbsp fresh lime juice
45 ml/3 tbsp white wine vinegar
50 ml/2 fl oz olive oil
¼ tsp ground cumin
½ tsp salt
⅛ tsp pepper
6 salmon steaks (100–225 g/4–8 oz each)

BLACK BEAN SALSA

1 large tomato, seeded and chopped
50 g/2 oz red onion, chopped
2 spring onions, chopped
1 clove garlic, crushed
2 jalapeño chillies, finely chopped
4 tbsp chopped fresh coriander
1 tsp ground cumin
30 ml/2 tbsp fresh lime juice
175 g/6 oz sweetcorn kernels, fresh or frozen
1 x 425-g/15-oz can black beans, rinsed and drained
salt and pepper to taste

~ Combine the lime juice, vinegar, oil, cumin, salt and pepper. Put the salmon in a shallow, non-reactive dish. Pour the marinade over the salmon. Turn salmon to be sure all sides are coated. Marinate the fish in the refrigerator for 1–2 hours, basting once or twice.

~ In the meantime make the salsa. Mix the tomato, red and spring onions, garlic, chillies, coriander, cumin and lime juice in a medium bowl. Put the corn in a small saucepan with about 50 ml/2 fl oz water. Bring to the boil and cook the corn until tender, 3–5 minutes. Drain most of the water, add the beans, and return pan to the heat. Cook just long enough to heat the beans, 2–3 minutes. Remove from heat and add to chopped vegetables. Add salt and pepper to taste and set aside.

~ Preheat grill. Place the salmon on a lightly greased grill pan. Grill about 12.5 cm/5 in from heat source. Turn once. Fish is done when the centre loses its redness but the flesh is still juicy, about 10 minutes per 2.5 cm/1 in of thickness.

GINGER-MANGO SALSA
makes about 350–450 g/12 oz–1 lb

Salsas made with mangoes and other fruits give an exotic touch to grilled fish, chicken and meat. If mangoes aren't available, substitute two papayas, or about 175 g/6 oz peeled and chopped peaches or nectarines. Because they aren't quite as juicy as mangoes, use a fork lightly to mash about 50 g/2 oz of the peaches or nectarines.

2 mangoes, peeled, stoned and diced
75 g/3 oz red onion, chopped
40 g/1½ oz red pepper, chopped
2 jalapeño chillies, seeds included, finely chopped
2 tsp grated fresh ginger
3 tbsp chopped fresh coriander
45 ml/3 tbsp fresh lime juice

~ Combine all ingredients. Stand for 30 minutes or so to allow flavours to blend.

GRILLED TROUT WITH DILL SAUCE

makes 4 servings
—

Some of the best methods of preparing trout are the simplest, starting with frying them over a campfire near the mountain stream where they were caught just minutes earlier. These trout are grilled – they can also be barbecued over charcoal – then served with a simple dill sauce.

DILL SAUCE

75 ml/5 tbsp soured cream
2 tbsp mayonnaise
1 tsp grated onion
5 ml/1 tsp fresh lemon juice
2 tsp dried dillweed

TROUT

4 trout (about 225 g/8 oz each), cleaned and boned
about 30 ml/2 tbsp olive oil
salt, pepper and paprika

~ Combine all the sauce ingredients. Leave to stand, refrigerated, for several hours to let the flavours develop.
~ Preheat the grill. Lay the fish, skin side down, on a lightly greased grill pan. Brush the fish with olive oil, then season with salt, pepper and paprika.
~ Put the trout in the oven, about 12.5 cm/5 in below the grill. Cook until the flesh loses its translucency but is still juicy, 6–8 minutes. Remove from grill and serve with the Dill Sauce.

CRAB-CORN CHILLIES RELLENOS

makes 4 main-course or 8 first-course servings
—

Chillies rellenos means stuffed chillies, and these are stuffed with a rich combination of crab, sweetcorn, soured cream and cheese. They are dipped in an egg white mixture, then fried until golden brown. Making chillies rellenos is both messy and time consuming, so set aside ample time for cooking and cleaning up. But what a delicious reward! Mild Anaheims – also known as California chillies – and the moderately hot poblanos are best, but the mild Cubanelle can also be substituted. (See notes on Roasting Chillies, page 26.)

8 whole Anaheim or poblano chillies
175 g/6 oz crabmeat, picked over for bits of shell
25 g/1 oz onion, chopped
175 g/6 oz sweetcorn kernels
2 tbsp chopped fresh coriander
120 ml/4 fl oz soured cream
1/8 tsp cayenne pepper
1 tsp salt
8 sticks Monterey Jack or Cheddar cheese
(2mm x 2.5 x 10 cm/1/8 x 1 x 4 in each)
about 65 g/2 1/2 oz cornmeal for dredging
4 eggs, separated
2 tbsp flour
1/4 tsp salt
oil for frying
salsa of your choice, to be served on the side

~ Char the skins of the chillies under the grill or on the barbecue, turning until the skins are mostly black. Don't expect the chillies to blacken evenly. As each chilli is done, remove it from the heat and place it in a bag. When all the chillies are done, let them steam in the bag for 10 minutes. It will make them easier to peel.
~ Remove the chillies from the bag and carefully peel off the blackened skin. Cut a slit down the length of the chilli and cut out the stalk, seeds and membranes. Set the chillies aside.
~ In a bowl, mix the crabmeat, onion, sweetcorn, soured cream, coriander, cayenne and salt. Put a stick of cheese in each chilli, then lightly stuff it with the crab mixture. If a chilli tears, press it back together. The egg coating will help hold it together when it is fried. Dredge each chilli in the cornmeal and shake off any excess. The chillies can be prepared in advance to this point and refrigerated.
~ In a medium bowl, beat the egg whites until soft peaks form. In a second bowl, lightly beat the egg yolks with the flour and salt. Fold the yolks into the whites.
~ Pour oil to a depth of 1 cm/1/2 in into a large frying pan and heat. While the oil is heating, dip 2 or 3 chillies into the egg mixture, using a spatula to cover any bare spots. Carefully place each chilli relleno into the hot oil. Cook only 2 or 3 at a time – they must not crowd each other. Cook, turning once, until golden on all sides, about 2 minutes. While the chillies are cooking, dip the next batch into the egg mixture.
~ Chillies rellenos can be kept in a warm oven until all are fried. Serve with salsa on the side.

◄ *Grilled Trout with Dill Sauce*

COCONUT PRAWNS

makes 4 main-course or 6 appetizer servings

Coconut prawns are a popular Hawaiian dish, made here with a tangy marinade and beer batter. It can be eaten as a finger food or a main course. Note that the prawns should be marinated for at least two hours before cooking. The prawns can be fried in advance, then quickly reheated in the oven. Coconut prawns are often served with traditional cocktail or tartare sauce, but try it with hot-sweet Apricot Dipping Sauce (page 22). Use the largest prawns you can find. Hoisin sauce is available in the oriental food sections of many supermarkets.

700 g/1½ lb large prawns
30 ml/2 tbsp Hoisin sauce
50 ml/2 fl oz fresh lime juice
1 tsp grated fresh ginger
175 g/6 oz flour
½ tsp salt
2 eggs
15 ml/1 tbsp vegetable oil
250 ml/8 fl oz flat beer
flour for dipping, about 50 g/2 oz
115 g/4½ oz desiccated coconut
oil for deep-frying

~ Shell and devein the prawns, leaving tails intact. Cut lengthways through the underside of the prawn so that the top half opens up like butterfly wings.

~ In a small bowl, combine the Hoisin sauce, lime juice and ginger. Put the prawns in a non-reactive bowl and toss with the marinade. Cover and refrigerate at least 2 hours, stirring once or twice.

~ The batter also benefits from being made in advance. Combine the flour and salt. In another bowl, lightly beat the eggs with a fork, then add the oil and beer. Stir the liquid into the flour until you have a slightly lumpy batter. Refrigerate the batter until you are ready to cook the prawns.

~ Drain the prawns. Stir the marinade into the batter. Lay out the ingredients in this order: the prawns, 50 g/2 oz flour in a small bowl or plate, the batter, the coconut in a bowl, and a large, clean plate.

~ Dip the prawns into the flour and shake off any excess – you want only a very light coating. Dip the prawns into the batter and let excess drip off. Roll the prawns in the coconut and pat on additional coconut if necessary. Put the prawns on the plate.

~ Turn on oven to very low temperature.

~ Pour 7.5 cm/3 in of oil into a heavy pan or wok. Heat oil to about 185°C/365°F (see notes on Deep-frying on page 14). Carefully put a few prawns in the oil so they do not crowd each other. Let them fry until golden brown, about 1 minute. Drain and put them on a platter in the warm oven. Let oil return to 185°C/365°F between batches.

POACHED HALIBUT WITH LEMON-ONION MARMALADE

makes 4 servings

A sweet-sour lemon marmalade, which can be made a day in advance, seasons this easy poached halibut.

LEMON-ONION MARMALADE
30 ml/2 tbsp olive oil
225 g/8 oz onions, coarsely chopped
1 small lemon
30 ml/2 tbsp balsamic vinegar
50 g/2 oz brown sugar
2 tsp grated fresh ginger

HALIBUT
4 halibut steaks, (150–175 g/5–6 oz each)
1 stick celery, including leaves, sliced
½ onion, sliced
½ lemon, unpeeled, thinly sliced
120 ml/4 fl oz dry white wine
several sprigs of parsley
1 bay leaf
½ tsp salt

~ Heat the oil in a large frying pan. Add the onions and sauté over a low heat until they are golden brown, 20–25 minutes. While the onion is cooking, grate lemon rind, being careful not to include white pith. Add lemon rind to onions while they are cooking. Remove pith from lemon. Slice lemon and remove seeds. Chop lemon slices and add to onions. Add vinegar, sugar and ginger. Simmer 5–10 minutes. Taste and add sugar if necessary.

~ Rinse the halibut. Place fish in a large frying pan or fish poacher. Add enough water to cover the fish by 2.5 cm/1 in. Remove halibut and set aside. To the water, add remaining ingredients except marmalade. Bring to the boil. Cover and boil 10 minutes to develop flavours. Carefully place the halibut in the water. Cover, reduce heat and simmer, 10 minutes per 2.5 cm/1 in of thickness. Remove and serve with the Lemon-onion Marmalade which should be warm.

WOK-SEARED ONO

makes 4 servings

*Wok-seared fish, cooked quickly over very high heat, so that the outside is well-done and the inside is still juicy,
is a staple of what's called the New Hawaiian Cuisine. This recipe borrows from techniques made famous by New Orleans' blackened
redfish, but is simpler and uses much less fat. Rather than a butter sauce, it is served with a fruit salsa, such as Ginger-mango Salsa
(page 92). You can use either a wok or a large frying pan. I prefer the wok because there is more surface to work with, and because
I can arrange thicker ends of unevenly cut fillets closer to the heat source. You can substitute firm-fleshed fish,
such as swordfish, shark or tuna, for ono. Bottled chilli oil, cooking oil infused with hot chillies and sometimes
other seasonings, is available in the oriental or sauce sections of many supermarkets.*

*8 ono or other firm-fleshed fish fillets, 5 mm–1 cm/
¼- to ½-in thick (about 75 g/3 oz each)
chilli oil
vegetable oil
fruit salsa of your choice*

~ Brush each fillet on both sides with the chilli oil.
Let the fish stand about 5 minutes, then brush
with additional oil. You'll probably use a teaspoon
or so per fillet.

~ Heat a wok. The wok must be very hot, so that
drops of water dance on the surface. Lightly brush
the walls of the wok with vegetable oil. You
should not use so much that it pools in the bottom
of the wok.

~ Working very quickly, place the fish fillets on
the walls of the wok, thickest part toward the
bottom. Cook just until the bottom is seared, 1
minute or a little longer. Quickly turn the fish and
cook until bottom is seared and inside has lost its
translucency but is still juicy, 1–2 minutes,
depending on the thickness of the fish.

~ Remove the fish and serve hot, 2 small pieces
per serving, with the fruit salsa.

CHIPOTLE-GRILLED PRAWNS

makes 4–6 main-course servings

Smokey chipotle chillies flavour the marinade for these spicy prawns. Skewers of grilled prawns can be served as an appetizer or a main course, with bowls of Salsa (page 29), Ginger-Mango Salsa (page 92), or Smokey Avocado Salsa (recipe follows) on the side.

50 ml/2 fl oz fresh lime juice
50 ml/2 fl oz orange juice
45 ml/3 tbsp olive oil
2 canned chipotle chillies, finely chopped, or 2 dried
4 tbsp chopped fresh coriander
700 g/1½ lb medium to large prawns, shelled and deveined

~ Combine all the ingredients except the prawns. If you use dried chipotles, pour on just enough boiling water to cover them, about 120 ml/4 fl oz. Let them soak 20–30 minutes, until they are soft. Drain water. Remove chilli stalks. Process the chillies in a food processor or blender with the orange and lime juices and the olive oil, then add coriander.

~ Put the prawns in a non-reactive dish. Pour marinade over prawns and toss so they are evenly coated. Marinate at least 30 minutes, turning once or twice.

~ If using wooden skewers, soak them in water 30 minutes to keep them from burning.

~ When the barbecue coals are almost ready, thread the prawns on the skewers. Don't jam the prawns together, or they will tend to cook unevenly.

~ Grill the prawns over glowing – not flaming – coals, about 2 minutes a side, until prawns curl up, turn white, and show bits of brown on the edges.

SMOKEY AVOCADO SALSA

makes about 275 g/10 oz

Unlike guacamole, where the avocado is mashed, this salsa uses diced avocado. It gets its smokey flavour from a chipotle chilli, a smoked jalapeño. In addition to crisps, it is excellent with chicken, beef and fish. If you make this salsa in advance, wait until serving time to cut up the avocado. Tip: if the avocados are not perfectly ripe, a few drops of avocado oil will improve the flavour of the salsa.

2 large, ripe avocados, peeled, stoned and diced
45 ml/3 tbsp fresh lime juice
40 g/1½ oz red onion, finely chopped
1 canned chipotle chilli, finely chopped
1 jalapeño or serrano chilli, finely chopped
1 medium tomato, seeded and chopped
1 clove garlic, pushed through a press
15 ml/1 tbsp olive oil
salt to taste

~ Mix the diced avocado with the lime juice. Stir in the remaining ingredients. Taste and adjust seasonings.

From breakfast breads and fruit-filled treats to soup and salad accompaniments, there is something for every occasion. The more traditional recipes include muffins, scones and sourdough waffles.

BREADS

BIG PECAN STICKY BUNS

makes 12 buns

*Enormous sticky buns are particularly popular in the Pacific Northwest, but
who can resist these rolls with their sweet combination of brown sugar, cinnamon and pecans?
As written this recipe will make twelve oversized but not huge buns. To make eight huge buns, make
each rectangle longer and skinnier – about 20 x 55 cm/8 x 22 in. Then cut each cylinder into four
rolls. For twenty-four small buns, make four rectangles, about 23 x 46 cm/9 x 18 in, and cut each
cylinder into 6 rolls. For twelve rolls, use three 20-cm/8-in square tins or two 20 x 30-cm/8 x 12-in
tins. If the rolls are too crowded, they will not rise and bake properly.*

DOUGH

175 g/6 oz plus 1 tbsp sugar
1 tsp salt
120 ml/4 fl oz milk
100 g/4 oz butter
120 ml/4 fl oz warm water, 40–45°C/105–115°F
2 packets dried yeast (7 g/¼ oz. each)
about 625 g/1¼ lb plain flour
2 eggs, lightly beaten with fork

FILLING

50 g/2 oz butter, softened to room temperature
175 g/6 oz brown sugar
1 tbsp ground cinnamon
100 g/4 oz chopped pecans

SYRUP

100 g/4 oz butter
250 g/9 oz brown sugar
30 ml/2 tbsp water
100 g/4 oz pecan halves

GLAZE

150 g/5 oz icing sugar
50 g/2 oz butter, very soft
1.25 ml/¼ tsp vanilla
about 30 ml/2 tbsp milk

~ To make the dough, heat 175 g/6 oz sugar, salt, milk and butter in a small saucepan. Heat until the butter is melted and sugar is dissolved. Set the mixture aside to cool. (Mixture must be cooler than 45°C/115°F or it will kill the yeast.)
~ Dissolve 1 tbsp sugar in the warm water. Add the yeast. Stand until it develops a thick head of foam, 5–10 minutes.
~ Put 450 g/1 lb flour in a large bowl. Add the yeast, then the milk–sugar mixture. Stir gently with a large spoon until the mixture is partially blended.
Add the eggs and stir until mixture is well blended. Add 50 g/2 oz of the remaining 100 g/4 oz flour. Stir. At this point, place the mixture onto a floured surface and begin kneading. Continue adding flour, a little at a time, as needed.
~ The dough should not be stiff, and can be just a little sticky. I usually use 625 g/1¼ lb flour in the dough, plus 25 g/1 oz to 50 g/2 oz periodically sprinkled on the kneading surface. Knead for a total of 8–10 minutes.
~ Place the dough in a large oiled bowl. Turn dough so all sides are coated with oil. Cover with a teatowel and set in a warm place to rise, until dough has doubled in volume, about 1¹/₂–2 hours.
~ Knock back the dough and knead lightly. Let the dough rest while you prepare filling and syrup. Then cut (don't tear) the dough in half. On a floured surface, roll each half into a rectangle of about 30 x 46 cm/12 x 18 in. Roll dough as thin as possible.
~ To make the filling, cream butter, sugar and

cinnamon. Sprinkle it evenly over each rectangle of dough. Sprinkle chopped pecans over filling. Starting with the short end, tightly roll each rectangle into a cylinder. Moisten the edge of the dough very slightly and seal cylinder. Trim uneven ends. Cut each cylinder into 6 equal slices.
~ To make the syrup, put butter, brown sugar and 30 ml/2 tbsp water in a small saucepan. Heat until the butter is melted and sugar is dissolved. Divide the syrup among the baking tins. Tilt and swirl the tins until the bottoms are evenly coated. Sprinkle pecan halves over the syrup.
~ Place 6 rolls, evenly spaced, in each pan. If any pecan pieces are not under a roll, slide them under one, otherwise they will go to waste.
~ Cover the baking tins and set them in a warm place for dough to rise. About 15 minutes before rising is completed, preheat the oven to 180°C/350°F/Gas Mark 4. When the dough has doubled in volume, 1–1¹/₂ hours, remove cover and put rolls in oven. Bake until sides are golden brown, about 30 minutes.
~ Invert immediately onto a platter, or rolls will stick to the pan. Make glaze by combining all the ingredients and spoon over rolls, letting some drizzle down the sides.

BLUEBERRY POPPY SEED MUFFINS

makes 12 large muffins

If you love blueberries but are tired of blueberry muffins that are overly sweet, here's a recipe for you. A bit of lemon rind cuts the sweetness, and poppy seeds give the muffins a nice texture.

225 g/8 oz flour
175 g/6 oz sugar
1½ tsp bicarbonate of soda
1 tsp baking powder
¼ tsp salt
¼ tsp grated nutmeg
2 tbsp poppy seeds
1 tsp grated lemon rind
50 g/2 oz butter, melted
175 ml/6 fl oz soured cream
75 ml/5 tbsp milk
1 egg, lightly beaten with fork
275 g/10oz blueberries, fresh or frozen

~ Preheat the oven to 200°C/400°F/Gas Mark 6. Lightly grease a 12-cup muffin or patty tin.
~ In a large bowl, mix the dry ingredients, including the lemon rind. In a separate bowl, combine the butter, soured cream and milk and mix well to cool the temperature of the butter. Mix in the egg. Pour the liquid ingredients into the dry ingredients and mix briefly by hand, about 15 seconds. Mixture should be slightly lumpy. Stir in the blueberries (thawed completely, if frozen).
~ Pour the mixture into the muffin or patty tin, filling them nearly to the brim. Bake until tops are golden and a knife inserted in the centre of a muffin comes out clean, 25–30 minutes.

CHILLI CHEESE BREAD

makes 1 loaf

*Chillies and Cheddar cheese flavour this hearty yeast bread, which goes
well with soup and salad. You can use canned green chillies as a shortcut to
roasting your own, but the flavour will not be as good.*

3 Anaheim, New Mexico green or poblano chillies
120 ml/4 fl oz milk
25 g/1 oz butter
½ tsp salt
7 g/¼ oz sachet dried yeast
75 ml/5 tbsp warm water, 40–45°C/105–115°F
1 tsp sugar
about 350 g/12 oz flour
1 egg, lightly beaten
100 g/4 oz mature Cheddar cheese, grated

~ Preheat the grill. Cut the chillies in half lengthways, remove stalks and seeds. Place under grill, skin side up, and cook until skin blisters and turns mostly dark brown or black. Remove from grill and place hot chillies in a bag or fold a pouch of foil around them to seal in the steam. Let them steam for 10 minutes, then peel off their skins and dice the chillies. This may always be done up to a day in advance of making the bread.

~ Scald the milk. Add the butter and salt to the milk and let the mixture cool. It's all right if the butter does not melt completely.

~ Dissolve the yeast in the warm water and add the sugar. Let yeast stand until it develops a foamy head, about 10 minutes. When the milk mixture has cooled to 45°C/115°F or less, combine it with the yeast mixture and pour the mixture into a large bowl. Stir in 100 g/4 oz flour. Stir in egg, cheese and chillies. Knead in 100 g/4 oz flour. Add about 50 g/2 oz, knead lightly, then tip the mixture onto a floured surface. The dough does not need to be well blended when you tip it out. Continue kneading, adding a little flour if necessary, until the dough has been kneaded for a total of 10 minutes.

~ Place the dough in a greased bowl, then turn the dough so all surfaces are lightly oiled. Cover the bowl and put it in a warm place for the dough to rise. When the dough has doubled in volume, 1–1¹/₂ hours, knock back and knead lightly. Let the dough rest while you lightly butter a 23-cm/9-in loaf tin. Shape the dough into a loaf and put it in the tin. Cover the tin and stand it in a warm place until the dough doubles in volume again. About 20 minutes before the dough has fully risen, preheat the oven to 190°C/375°F/Gas Mark 5.

~ Bake the bread until the top is golden and sounds hollow when you tap it. This will take about 30 minutes.

GINGER MUFFINS

makes 12 muffins

*Warm and spicy, these old-fashioned muffins are a real breakfast treat.
Crystallized ginger is available in the spice section of most supermarkets. Serve
the muffins with homemade Apple Butter (recipe follows).*

225 g/8 oz plain flour
1½ tsp bicarbonate of soda
1½ tsp ground ginger
1½ tsp ground cinnamon
3 tbsp finely chopped crystallized ginger
175 g/6 oz butter, melted
175 g/6 oz brown sugar
175 g/6 oz molasses
2 eggs, lightly beaten with fork
1 tsp grated lemon rind
75 ml/5 tbsp milk

~ Preheat the oven to 180°C/350°F/Gas
Mark 4. Lightly oil a 12-cup muffin or patty tin.
~ Combine the flour, bicarbonate of soda,
ginger, cinnamon and crystallized ginger.
~ In a separate bowl, mix the remaining
ingredients. Mix the liquid ingredients into the
flour mixture. Pour this mixture into the muffin
or patty tin, filling to just below the top. Bake
until a knife inserted in the centre of a muffin
comes out clean, about 20 minutes.

APPLE BUTTER
makes about 250 ml/8 fl oz

*This recipe makes just enough for a special
brunch, so you don't have to worry about
preserving it. It's easy to make and can
simmer on the cooker while muffins are
baking, or can be made several days ahead.*

*2 large or 3 small cooking apples, such as
Bramley's*
120 ml/4 fl oz water
100 g/4 oz brown sugar
1 tsp ground cinnamon
⅛ tsp ground cloves
⅛ tsp ground allspice

~ Peel and core the apples and cut them into
chunks. Put the apples in a small saucepan with
120 ml/4 fl oz water. Bring the water to the
boil, then reduce heat and simmer, stirring
occasionally. As the apples soften, mash them
lightly with a fork or back of a spoon.

~ When the apples are cooked to the
consistency of purée, add sugar and spices.
Taste and add more sugar if necessary,
depending on the tartness of the apples. Cook
until sugar is dissolved.

SOURDOUGH FRENCH BREAD

makes 2 loaves

The most popular use of sourdough is in a dense, crusty French bread. The best French breads from commercial bakeries with their speciality ovens are hard to copy in a home kitchen, but this recipe will come close. The only speciality item you will need is a pizza stone or enough ceramic tiles to line your oven rack.

1 cupful sourdough starter (page 110)
350 ml/12 fl oz warm water
(40–45°C/105–115°F)
about 700 g/1½ lb plain flour
2 tsp salt
2 tsp sugar
cornmeal
1 tsp cornflour

~ The night before baking, prepare the sponge. Mix the starter, the warm water and 450 g/1 lb flour in a large bowl. Cover loosely and leave it in a warm place overnight. (Don't forget to replenish the starter pot with 100 g/4 oz flour and 250 ml/8 fl oz water.)

~ The next morning, the sponge should be bubbly and should have risen somewhat. Mix in the salt and sugar. Then add about 175 g/6 oz flour. Mix it until most of the flour is incorporated, then turn the dough out on a floured surface. Knead the dough, adding flour as needed, for about 10 minutes, until you have a stiff dough. Place the dough in a greased bowl and turn it over so all surfaces are lightly oiled. Loosely cover the bowl and leave it in a warm place to rise until it has doubled in bulk, 1½–2 hours.

~ Knock back the dough. Knead briefly. Cut (do not tear) the dough in half. Roll each piece into a loaf, then gently roll it back and forth,

elongating it. Place each loaf on a piece of cardboard, a rimless baking sheet, or the underside of a baking sheet that has been sprinkled with cornmeal. Cover loaves with a towel and put them in a warm place to rise until they have almost doubled in bulk, 1–1½ hours.

~ About 20 minutes before dough has finished rising, preheat the oven to 200°C/400°F/Gas Mark 6. Place tiles or pizza stone on top shelf and let them heat. Boil 450 ml/¾ pt water, pour into a shallow baking tin, and put pan of water on bottom shelf of oven. (The steam will increase the crustiness of the bread.) Sprinkle cornmeal on the heated tiles or pizza stone.

~ In a small pan, mix the cornflour and 120 ml/4 fl oz water. Bring it to the boil, then let it cool slightly.

~ When bread has finished rising, use a very sharp knife or razor blade to cut several 1-cm/½-in-deep diagonal slashes in the top of each loaf. Brush top and sides of each loaf with cornflour-water mixture.

~ You are now ready to put the bread in the oven. I find that sliding the loaves onto the hot tiles or pizza stone – without twisting or deflating the dough – to be the most difficult step. Carefully slide the loaves off the cardboard or baking sheet onto the tile or pizza stone.

~ Bake until the bread is golden brown and sounds hollow when tapped, 30–40 minutes.

SEED BREAD

makes two 23-cm/9-in loaves

To toast sesame seeds and wheatgerm, put each into a small frying pan over medium heat. Shake the pan occasionally so seeds do not scorch. Cook until they brown lightly.

2 x 7 g/¼ oz packets dried yeast
1 tsp sugar
120 ml/4 fl oz warm water, 40–45°C/105–115°F
300 ml/½ pt warm milk
60 ml/4 tbsp olive oil
100 g/4 oz honey
2 tsp salt
175 g/6 oz wholemeal flour
50 g/2 oz toasted wheatgerm
3 tbsp toasted sesame seeds
50 g/2 oz roasted sunflower seeds
about 400 g/14 oz plain white flour

~ Dissolve yeast and sugar in the warm water. Let the yeast build up a foamy head.

~ Mix the milk, olive oil, honey and salt. Put the wholemeal flour in a large bowl. Stir in the milk mixture. When yeast is ready, add it to the bowl. Stir in wheatgerm, sesame and sunflower seeds. Add 350 g/12 oz white flour, 100 g/4 oz at a time. When dough becomes too thick to stir in the bowl, tip it out onto a floured surface and knead. Knead the dough for a total of 10 minutes.

~ Put the dough in a large greased bowl. Turn so entire surface is lightly oiled. Cover it loosely and set it in a warm place. When dough has doubled in volume, about 1½ hours, knock back and knead it lightly. Cut (do not tear) the dough in half. Let it rest while you prepare tins.

~ Grease two 23-cm/9-in loaf tins. Gently shape each mound of dough and put it in a loaf tin. Put in a warm place and loosely cover them. Twenty minutes before dough has finished rising, preheat the oven to 180°C/350°F/Gas Mark 4. When dough has doubled in volume, 1 hour or so, put the loaves in the oven and bake until golden.

Seed Bread ➤

PORTUGUESE SWEET BREAD

makes 1 loaf

Portuguese colonists brought a version of this bread to Hawaii, where it is still popular. It is a slightly sweet, eggy bread usually eaten at breakfast. It was originally an Easter bread, but a modified version is now eaten year-round. This bread is flavoured with lemon rind and nutmeg. You may also add 75 g/3 oz coarsely chopped unsalted macadamia nuts.

50 g/2 oz butter
120 ml/4 fl oz milk, scalded
100 g/4 oz sugar
1.25 ml/¼ tsp vanilla essence
1½ tsp grated lemon rind
1 tsp grated nutmeg
¼ tsp salt
7 g/¼ oz sachet dried yeast
50 ml/2 fl oz warm water, 40–45°C/105–115°F
about 350 g/12 oz flour
3 eggs

~ Put the butter in the hot milk and let it melt slowly. It does not have to melt completely. Mix in the sugar (setting 1 tsp sugar aside for the yeast), vanilla, lemon rind, nutmeg and salt. Let the milk mixture cool.
~ Dissolve the yeast in the warm water and add the reserved 1 tsp sugar. Let the yeast develop a foamy head, 5–10 minutes.
~ Mix the milk mixture with 100 g/4 oz flour in a large bowl. Add the yeast mixture. Mix well. Beat 2 of the eggs with a fork and stir them into the batter. Add the remaining flour, stirring, then kneading. Turn the mixture out on a floured surface and continue kneading, adding flour as needed, for 7–8 minutes. This is a soft dough, and too much flour will make it too stiff.
~ Put the dough in an oiled bowl and turn the dough so all surfaces are oiled. Cover loosely and set dough in a warm place to rise. Let it rise so it is a little more than doubled in volume, 1½–2 hours. Knock dough back and knead lightly. Let it rest while you butter a 23-cm/9-in round cake tin.
~ Place the dough in the cake tin. Cover loosely and let it rise until it has doubled in volume, about 1½ hours. About 20 minutes before rising is completed, preheat the oven to 180°C/350°F/Gas Mark 4. When the bread has risen, beat the third egg with a fork. Gently brush it over the top of the bread.
~ Bake the bread until top is browned and the loaf sounds hollow when tapped, about 35 minutes.

SOURDOUGH STARTER

Sourdough bread is a distinctive product of the California Gold Rush of 1849, most likely the result of bread dough being left out and forgotten for several days. The sour taste that the fermented dough gave to bread was hugely popular. It became so ubiquitous in mining camps from California to Alaska that prospectors were often called sourdoughs.

Sourdough bread remains enormously popular in the West. When my sister moved to Florida, she demanded that anyone visiting her from California bring sourdough bread with them.

Sourdough is a batter that is allowed to ferment and draw in wild yeasts from the air. The fermented batter is added to bread dough, giving it a pleasantly sour flavour. Most people associate sourdough with a dense, crusty French bread, but it can be used to flavour all kinds of breads, from waffles to muffins to corn bread.

A pot of starter takes several days to a week to ferment and develop its sour flavour before it is used for the first time. When it is ready, a portion of the starter is mixed with flour and water to make a sponge. The sponge must sit overnight, and is the heart of the bread that is baked in the morning. Meanwhile, the starter is refreshed with additional flour and water. Maintaining a pot of sourdough starter is not difficult, and it demands little care after the initial fermenting – just once-a-week feedings. Aficionados keep the same pot of starter going for years, and swear that the flavour keeps improving, even after many years. You can buy sourdough starter in some specialist food shops, but making your own starter is easy.

250 ml/8 fl oz low-fat milk, scalded
250 ml/8 fl oz hot water
1 tbsp sugar
7 g/¼ oz sachet dried yeast
275 g/10 oz plain flour

~ Mix the milk, water and sugar. When the temperature has cooled to between 40° and 45°C/105° and 115°F, add the yeast. When the yeast mixture has developed a foamy head, add it to the flour. Mix well. Place the bowl in a warm place, between 28° and 38°C/80° and 100°, like the top of the water heater or under a light. The bowl should be covered with a partly askew lid so it can gather airborne yeasts. By the next day, the mixture should be bubbly and have a slightly sour smell. The mixture may separate into a curd-like substance and a watery liquid. This is normal. Just periodically stir the watery liquid back in. If the liquid turns pink or green, however, throw it away and start again. The mixture is ready to use when it develops a good sour smell, usually 3–5 days.

~ To bake sourdough bread, you need to prepare the sponge at least 6 hours in advance. Preferably you should do this the night before you plan to bake. To make the sponge, use ½ cup–1 cup starter, and add flour and water, according to your recipe. The sponge must stand in a warm place at least 6 hours; follow the recipe from this point.

~ You must also replenish the remaining starter. Do this by stirring in as much flour and water as you took out in starter. For example, if you removed 1 cup starter for use in the sponge, stir 100 g/4 oz flour and 250 ml/8 fl oz water back into the starter pot. The starter should sit in a warm place at least 6–8 hours until it is bubbly. If you bake every day, simply leave the starter pot out, perhaps at the back of the cooker. If you do not bake every day, keep the starter pot in the refrigerator, tightly covered, after it has been replenished and has had at least 6 hours to ferment in a warm place.

~ The starter is best kept in a glass, pottery or rigid plastic container with a tight-fitting lid. If you do not bake regularly, you should refresh the starter every week or two. To do this, remove 1 cup of starter; discard the rest. To the starter, add 250 ml/8 fl oz water and 100 g/4 oz flour. Let the starter sit in a warm place for 6 hours or longer, then cover it and return it to the refrigerator to store.

CRANBERRY SCONES

makes 6 servings

—

The West Coast, in its never-ending quest for the perfect breakfast breads, has seized on scones. But instead of the traditional currants, bakers flavour them with everything from raspberries to cinnamon-sugar streusel to cheese and herbs. Here they are flavoured with dried cranberries from the inland valleys of the Pacific Northwest.

225 g/8 oz flour
1½ tsp baking powder
½ tsp bicarbonate of soda
½ tsp salt
3 tbsp sugar
1 tsp grated orange rind
50 g/2 oz butter, melted
175 ml/6 fl oz buttermilk
100 g/4 oz dried cranberries
15 ml/1 tbsp milk or single cream

~ Preheat the oven to 200°C/400°F/Gas Mark 6.
~ Combine the dry ingredients and the grated orange rind. In a small bowl, combine the melted butter and buttermilk. Pour the milk mixture into the flour mixture and stir by hand until mixed. Stir in the dried cranberries.
~ Roll the dough into a ball. On a floured surface, flatten it into a circle. You can roll it out with a floured rolling-pin, but the dough should be soft enough that you can pat it out by hand. Roll or pat the dough until it is about 1 cm/½ in thick, and forms a circle with a diameter of about 20 cm/8 in. Cut the circle into 6 or 8 wedges. Carefully transfer the wedges to an ungreased baking sheet.
~ Brush the tops of the wedges with milk or cream and bake until tops are lightly browned, 10–12 minutes. Serve warm with butter and jam or honey if desired.

FOCACCIA

makes 6–8 servings

Focaccia is a flat, dense bread, similar to pizza dough. It is topped with olive oil, garlic, rosemary and Parmesan cheese. Serve it warm, cut in wedges, with a shallow dish of extra-virgin olive oil for dipping. Focaccia is a perfect accompaniment to soup or salad, or with antipasto. Some people sprinkle about 1 teaspoon of coarse salt over the top of the focaccia before baking.

1 tsp sugar
7 g/¼ oz sachet dried yeast
250 ml/8 fl oz warm water, 40–45°C/105–115°F
350 g/12 oz plain flour
2 tsp salt
90 ml/6 tbsp olive oil, plus extra for bowl
cornmeal
2 garlic cloves, crushed
2 tsp chopped fresh rosemary or 1 tsp dried
3–4 tbsp freshly grated Parmesan cheese

~ Dissolve the sugar and yeast in the water. Let it stand until the mixture is foamy, 5–10 minutes.
~ Mix the flour and salt in a large bowl. Stir in 45 ml/3 tbsp of the olive oil and the yeast mixture until the liquids are mostly incorporated. Turn the dough onto a lightly floured surface and knead for about 10 minutes. Put the dough in an oiled bowl, and turn the dough so it is oiled on all sides. Cover the bowl with a teatowel and set it in a warm place.
~ When the dough has doubled in size, after 1–1¹/₂ hours, knock back. Knead it lightly. Put it back in the bowl to rise again.
~ Preheat the oven to 200°C/400°F/Gas Mark 6. Sprinkle cornmeal on a large baking sheet or pizza stone.
~ After the dough has again doubled in size, knock back. Leave it in one ball for a large focaccia, about the size of a cookie baking sheet, or cut it in half for two 25 cm/10-in circles of bread. On a lightly floured surface, roll the dough out to 1-cm/¹/₂-in thickness. Place it on the baking sheet.
~ With your fingertips, poke shallow indentations in the top of the dough. Pour the remaining 45 ml/3 tbsp olive oil over the top

and spread it evenly, allowing some of it to pool in the indentations. Sprinkle the garlic over the bread and press it lightly into the surface. Sprinkle the rosemary and Parmesan over the bread.
~ Bake until the bread is lightly browned, anything from 18–22 minutes.

ALASKAN BLUEBERRY SOURDOUGH WAFFLES

makes 6–8 18-cm/7-in round waffles

This is a favourite dish in Alaska, where blueberries grow wild, and some sourdough starters are said to be over 100 years old. In this recipe, some of the sponge is used to replenish the sourdough starter pot. To make pancakes instead of waffles, decrease the butter to 25 g/1 oz and sugar to 2 tbsp.

1 cupful sourdough starter (page 110)
450 ml/¾ pt warm water, 40–45°C/105–115°F
275 g/10 oz flour
2 eggs, lightly beaten with fork
50 g/2 oz butter, melted
¼ tsp salt
1 tsp bicarbonate of soda
3 tbsp sugar
30–60 ml/2–4 tbsp milk
175 g/6 oz blueberries, fresh or frozen

~ The night before making the waffles, make the sponge. Combine the starter, warm water and flour. Return 1 cup of the new mixture back to the starter pot. Let both mixtures stand in a warm place overnight, loosely covered. In the morning, stir the starter, put a lid on it, and return it to the refrigerator.

~ To the new sponge, add eggs, butter, salt, soda and sugar. Add milk until batter is of desired consistency; this makes a fairly thin batter. Stir in the blueberries (thawed, if frozen).

~ Make waffles as directed in your waffle grid manufacturer's instructions. Batter should cover about ²/₃ of the waffle grid. Be sure the blueberries are spread out, not in a pile where you poured the batter. Check waffles when steam stops coming from the waffle maker. If the waffle maker doesn't open easily, let the waffle cook another minute or so. Be sure the waffle iron has reheated before you pour on the batter for the next waffle.

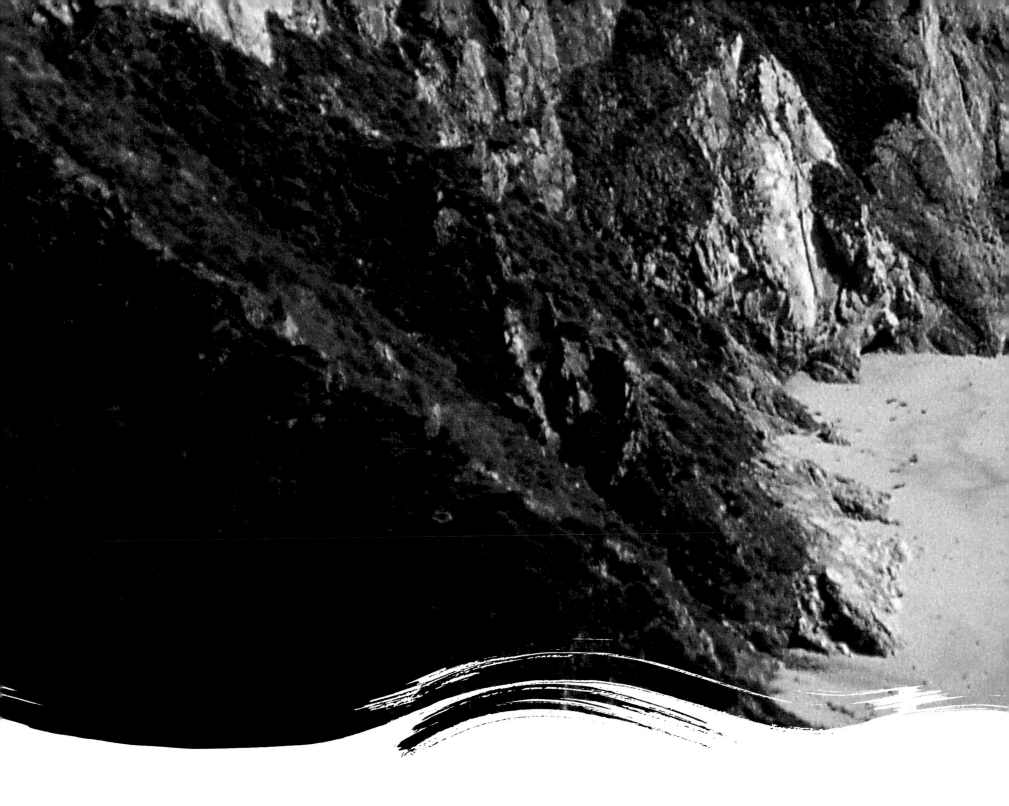

An irresistible collection of sweet delights from Baked Pears and
Grilled Fruit to Chocolate Espresso Mousse and Orange
Crème Brûlée. Tempting and delicious, they capture
the very essence of Pacific Rim cooking.

DESSERTS

RASPBERRY LEMON TART

makes 8 servings

This delicious tart has a custard base flavoured with California lemons and topped with raspberries from Oregon. Instead of the tart pastry given below you can use your favourite pastry recipe.

TART PASTRY

150 g/5 oz flour
¼ tsp salt
2 tbsp sugar
100 g/4 oz cold butter
1 egg yolk, beaten with 30 ml/2 tbsp iced water

FILLING

1 tbsp cornflour
15 ml/1 tbsp cold milk
250 ml/8 fl oz hot milk
75 g/3 oz sugar
2 egg yolks
2 tsp grated lemon rind
30 ml/2 tbsp fresh lemon juice
15 g/½ oz butter
225–275 g/8–10 oz raspberries, picked over

~ Combine the flour, salt and sugar. Cut in the butter. Mix in the egg-water mixture by hand until the dough forms a ball. If the mixture is too dry, add a little more ice water.

~ The dough will be easier to handle if it is rolled in cling film and allowed to rest in the refrigerator for 30 minutes.

~ Preheat the oven to 180°C/350°F/Gas Mark 4. Roll out the dough on a floured surface.

Carefully place it in a 23-cm/9-in flan tin and trim off the rough edges.

~ Prick the case with a fork in several places. Bake until lightly golden, 15–20 minutes. If pastry bubbles up while baking, prick it with a fork. If you use baking beans, remove them during last 5 minutes of baking to let case brown. Leave pastry to cool.

~ Mix the cornflour and cold milk to make a paste. Put it in the top of a double saucepan with the hot milk and sugar. Whisk until smooth. Heat the mixture over simmering water, stirring constantly, until it thickens slightly. Remove from heat.

~ Beat the egg yolks until they are thick and lemon-coloured. Add a little of the hot milk mixture to the eggs, whisking constantly, to raise the temperature of the eggs gradually. Then pour the egg yolks into the remaining milk mixture, whisking until smooth. Heat over simmering water, stirring constantly, until mixture thickens and coats the back of a spoon.

~ Remove custard from heat. Stir in lemon rind, lemon juice and butter until butter is melted and mixture is well blended. Pour the custard into the cooled pastry case. When the custard is almost set, arrange raspberries in concentric circles on top of the custard.

MANGO CHEESECAKE

makes 12–16 servings

Mangoes thrive in the tropics, and are favourites in Mexico and Hawaii. Here we've married the delicate flavour of mangoes with tangy cheesecake in a coconut-digestive biscuit base. The flavour is best if the cheesecake is made 12–24 hours in advance.

CRUST

100 g/4 oz digestive biscuit crumbs
25 g/1 oz desiccated coconut
3 tbsp sugar
50 g/2 oz melted butter

FILLING

700 g/1½ lb cream cheese, softened to room temperature
225 g/8 oz sugar
350 g/12 oz mango purée, slightly chunky (about 2 mangoes)
250 ml/8 fl oz soured cream
4 eggs

~ Preheat the oven to 180°C/350°F/Gas Mark 4.

~ Combine the crumbs, coconut and sugar. Stir in the melted butter. Press crumbs into bottom and slightly up sides of 25-cm/10-in springclip tin. Bake until base just starts to brown, 9–11 minutes. Remove and leave to cool.

~ Reduce oven temperature to 170°C/325°F/Gas Mark 3.

~ Cream the cream cheese and sugar. Add mango purée, soured cream and eggs, and beat until well blended. Pour filling into cooled base.

~ Bake until the centre is set, 60–70 minutes. It is natural for the filling to shrink, but you can reduce cracking by turning off the oven, opening the door, and letting the cheesecake cool gradually, near but not in the heat. Once it has cooled to room temperature, refrigerate it.

Mango Cheesecake ➤

CHOCOLATE ESPRESSO MOUSSE

makes 6–8 servings

In this recipe, there is a much higher proportion of coffee flavouring than usual. Because of the addition of whipped cream, this mousse is lighter than the traditional dense mousse. It is very pretty when served in large goblets with a dollop of whipped cream and chocolate shavings.

50 ml/2 fl oz milk
2 tbsp espresso powder
100 g/4 oz bittersweet or plain chocolate
75 g/3 oz sugar
4 eggs, separated
150 ml/¼ pt double cream

~ Scald the milk. Dissolve the espresso powder in the milk. In the top of a double saucepan over simmering water, melt the chocolate. Add the milk-espresso mix and the sugar. Whisk until the sugar has dissolved and the mixture is totally smooth.

~ In a small bowl, beat the egg yolks until they are thick and lemon-coloured. Add a little of the hot chocolate to the eggs to raise their temperature gradually. Then pour the eggs into the remaining chocolate mixture. Whisk until smooth. Cook about 3 minutes longer, stirring constantly. Remove from heat and leave to cool, about 10 minutes.

~ In a medium bowl, beat the egg whites until soft peaks form. Gently fold in the chocolate mixture with a metal spoon.

~ In a large bowl, beat the cream until soft peaks form. Gently fold in the chocolate mixture. Pour into a large serving bowl or individual goblets or serving dishes. Chill at least 4 hours.

◄ *Chocolate Espresso Mousse*

BLACKBERRY ICE CREAM

makes about 1.5–1.75 litres/2½–3 pt

You don't have to venture far into the country to see blackberries growing wild along the roads of Oregon and Washington. The vines grow aggressively in city and country alike, their fruit a treat available for the picking.

275 g/10 oz blackberries
225 g/8 oz sugar
350 ml/12 fl oz double cream
350 ml/12 fl oz milk
1 tsp vanilla essence
3 egg yolks

~ Put the blackberries in a small bowl with 50 g/2 oz of the sugar. Crush the blackberries. Leave them to stand while you make the custard.

~ Scald the cream and milk. (This is best done in a microwave oven or in the top of a double saucepan so the milk proteins don't sink to the bottom and scorch.) Add the vanilla and 175 g/6 oz sugar. Put in top of double saucepan over boiling water. In a small bowl, whisk the egg yolks. Add a little of the hot cream to the eggs, whisking constantly, so that you raise the temperature of the eggs gradually. Then add the eggs to the cream. Continue cooking the custard in the double saucepan until mix thickens slightly and coats the back of a spoon.

~ Remove the custard from heat and leave to cool slightly, then refrigerate it before adding the crushed blackberries.

~ Put in an ice cream maker and make according to manufacturer's instructions.

APPLE HAZELNUT BARS

makes 16 5-cm/2-in squares, or 6–8 dessert bars

The bar is a little messy to be eaten out of the hand like a biscuit. I prefer it served on a dessert plate with vanilla ice cream.

CRUST
75 g/3 oz butter, softened
50 g/2 oz brown sugar
½ tsp vanilla
⅛ tsp salt
75 g/3 oz flour
15 ml/1 tbsp water
40 g/1½ oz finely ground toasted hazelnuts

FILLING
5 tart apples
150 g/5 oz sugar
½ tsp ground cinnamon
1 tbsp cornflour

TOPPING
3 tbsp brown sugar
3 tbsp flour
25 g/1 oz butter
½ tsp ground cinnamon

~ Preheat the oven to 180°C/350°F/Gas Mark 4. Grease an 20-cm/8-in square baking pan.

~ To make the crust, cream the butter and sugar. Beat in the vanilla and salt. Add the flour, water and ground hazelnuts; mix well. Pat mixture into bottom of baking tin. Bake until set and lightly browned, 12–15 minutes. Remove from the oven and let it cool.

~ To make the filling, peel and core the apples, then slice them thinly. Put the apples, sugar and cinnamon in a small saucepan. Cook over low heat about 8 minutes. Pour off about 30 ml/2 tbsp of the pan juices. Mix in cornflour to make a paste. Mix paste back into apples and cook until mixture thickens, about 1 minute. Pour apples over crust.

~ Mix topping ingredients and crumble over apples. Bake 15–20 minutes. Cool until just barely warm, then slice into squares or bars as desired.

PINEAPPLE PIE

makes 8 servings

—

A tangy cream cheese layer is the surprise in this sweet pineapple pie. A large pineapple produces about 350 g/12 oz of chopped fruit. If you come up a little short, you can make up the difference with canned crushed pineapple. If you have a little extra, you can add a few tablespoons of pineapple to the cream cheese filling.

23-cm/9-in pastry case, unbaked
(use tart pastry on page 116)

CREAM CHEESE FILLING
75 g/3 oz sugar
175 g/6 oz cream cheese, softened to room temperature
50 ml/2 fl oz soured cream
1 egg

PINEAPPLE FILLING
about 350 g/12 oz fresh pineapple, chopped
175 g/6 oz sugar
3 tbsp cornflour

~ Put the chopped pineapple in a colander to drain for 1 hour.
~ Preheat the oven to 180°C/350°F/Gas Mark 4. Have the unbaked pastry case ready. Cream the sugar and cream cheese, then beat in the soured cream and egg. Spread cream cheese filling in bottom of case. Bake until set, 15–20 minutes.
~ In a small saucepan, mix the drained pineapple and 175 g/6 oz sugar. Cook over medium heat. The pineapple will produce more juices, but watch carefully and stir frequently for the first minute or so to be sure the pineapple doesn't scorch while the pan is still dry. Cook until the sugar is dissolved and juices bubble. Pour off about 45 ml/3 tbsp of the pan juices and mix, a little at a time, into the cornstarch to make a smooth paste. Add the paste to the pineapple and cook until mixture thickens, about 30 seconds. Spread in pastry case over cream cheese filling. Bake until pastry is browned and filling is set, about 40 minutes.

APPLE SPICE CAKE

makes 8–10 servings

—

From Washington State's Yakima Valley, which calls itself "the Nation's Fruit Bowl", comes the inspiration for this homey cake. Apple purée, walnuts and spices provide an old-fashioned but oh-so-good flavour, topped by a simple cream cheese icing. If shop-bought apple purée seems thin and runny, put 350–400 g/12–14 oz apple purée in a small saucepan and cook it until thick, then measure 225 g/8 oz. If a picnic in the apple orchards takes your fancy, leave the cake in its baking tin and ice it, then take it along still in the tin.

175 g/6 oz sugar
175 g/6 oz brown sugar
100 g/4 oz butter, softened to room temperature
3 eggs
120 ml/4 fl oz buttermilk
225 g/8 oz thick apple purée
250 g/9 oz flour
1½ tsp bicarbonate of soda
½ tsp salt
2 tsp ground cinnamon
1 tsp grated nutmeg
1 tsp ground allspice
100 g/4 oz walnuts, chopped

ICING
175 g/6 oz cream cheese, softened to room temperature
50 g/2 oz unsalted butter, softened to room temperature
1 tsp vanilla essence
275 g/10 oz icing sugar
(measured before sifting)

~ Preheat the oven to 180°C/350°F/Gas Mark 4. Lightly grease and flour a 23 x 33-cm/9 x 13-in baking tin.
~ In a large bowl, cream the sugars and butter. Add the eggs, buttermilk and apple purée and mix together well.
~ In a separate bowl, mix the flour, bicarbonate of soda, salt and spices. Gradually beat the flour mixture into the butter mixture. Stir in the walnuts. Pour into baking tin.
~ Bake until a knife inserted in the centre of the cake comes out clean, about 35 minutes. Cool on a wire rack, then invert on platter.
~ Combine the icing ingredients and beat until smooth. The cake must be completely cool when you ice it, or the icing will turn runny.

COCONUT FLAN

makes 4–6 servings

Flan is a traditional Mexican dessert, made tropical here with coconut and coconut milk. The rich dessert is deceptively easy to make. First, the bottom of each ramekin is coated with caramelized sugar. Then a simple coconut custard is added and baked. The flan must cool at least three hours, but it's best when it's made a day in advance. Then it is inverted on a serving plate, so that the caramelized sugar becomes the topping. You will need four 250 ml/8 fl oz ramekins or six 175 ml/6 fl oz ramekins. If you buy a 400-g/14-oz. or 425-g/15-oz. can of coconut milk, make up the difference with whole milk.

225–275 g/8–10 oz sugar
6 eggs
1 tsp vanilla essence
450 ml/¾ pt coconut milk
40 g/1½ oz desiccated coconut

~ Preheat the oven to 170°C/325°F/Gas Mark 3.
~ Put 100 g/4 oz sugar (or 175 g/6 oz if you are using 6 ramekins) in a frying pan over medium-high heat. Cook, stirring frequently, until the sugar liquefies and becomes an amber syrup. Working quickly, pour the syrup into the ramekins, tilting the ramekins so the bottoms are coated as evenly as possible. (Because the syrup hardens quickly, this process is easier if one person pours and a second person makes sure each ramekin is coated. However, the syrup will redistribute itself while the custard is cooking, so don't worry if it's not perfectly even.)
~ Beat the eggs, vanilla and remaining 100 g/ 4 oz sugar in a medium bowl. Mix in the coconut milk, then the coconut. Pour the mixture into the ramekins.
~ Place the ramekins into 1 or 2 large baking tins. Pour hot water into the tins around the ramekins, taking care not to spill any into the custard. The water should be at least halfway up the outsides of the ramekins, but at least 2.5 cm/ 1 in below the tops.
~ Bake until the custard is set, about 50 minutes. A cocktail stick inserted in the centre of the custard should come out clean. Refrigerate at least 3 hours.
~ To serve, run a knife around the edge of each flan to loosen it. Place a small serving plate upside down over the top of each ramekin. Then invert the plate and ramekin. The flan should slide out onto the plate. If it does not, gently pry it loose with a knife.

—

ORANGE CREME BRULEE

makes 6 servings

—

*Crème brûlée is probably the richest of all custard desserts. With its crunchy
sugar crust, it is a little more complicated than some, but still not a difficult
dessert to make, compared to the elegance of the final product. This crème brûlée is
steeped with grated orange rind. It can be made up to a day in advance but
no more, or the sugar crust will start to dissolve.*

450 ml/¾ pt double cream
450 ml/¾ pt single cream
grated rind of 2 oranges (no white pith)
4 eggs
4 egg yolks
225 g/8 oz sugar
30 ml/2 tbsp Grand Marnier
6 tbsp brown sugar, or more as needed

~ Preheat the oven to 170°C/325°F/Gas Mark 3.
~ Combine both the creams and orange rind in
a heavy saucepan. Warm until the cream is
steaming but not boiling, about 82°C/180°F.
Cover pan and turn off heat. Let cream steep for
15 minutes to develop orange flavour.

~ Lightly beat the eggs, egg yolks, sugar and
Grand Marnier together. Add a little hot cream
to the mix and stir well. Continue adding the
cream, a little at a time so its temperature
doesn't curdle the eggs. Stir well. Strain the
custard to remove the orange rind.
~ Pour the custard into six 250-ml/8-fl oz
ramekins. Put the ramekins in 1 or 2 roasting
tins. Pour hot water into the roasting tin around
the ramekins, taking care not to spill any water
into the custard, until the water reaches about
halfway up the sides of the ramekins. Cover the
pan loosely with foil. Bake until custard is firm
around edges, about 50 minutes.
~ Cool the custard. When the custard is
completely cold, preheat the grill. Sprinkle

about 1 tablespoon of brown sugar over the top
of each custard. If the ramekins are wide and
shallow, they will require a little more sugar.
The sugar must completely cover the top of
the custard.
~ Put the custards on a baking sheet under the
grill. They should cook until the sugar dissolves
and caramelizes, a process that can take as little
as 45 seconds or as long as several minutes. The
custards must be watched closely so they do not
burn, but a small burnt spot or two adds to the
flavour. Let the custards cool again before
serving.

PINEAPPLE ANGEL FOOD CAKE

makes 12–16 servings

Crushed pineapple adds a tropical touch to this classic cake, newly popular because of its low fat and cholesterol content. A recipe for a glaze is included, but it's only for aesthetic purposes to cover the cake's bald spots if it is served plain. The cake is sweet enough that it doesn't need icing. Serve it with fresh fruit or a tart sorbet.

1 x 450-g/16-oz. can crushed pineapple,
packed in juice
12 large egg whites
150 g/5 oz cake flour, sifted
400 g/14 oz sugar
1½ tsp cream of tartar
½ tsp salt
10 ml/2 tsp vanilla essence

PINEAPPLE GLAZE
225 g/8 oz icing sugar, sifted
25 g/1 oz butter, very soft
about 45 ml/3 tbsp pineapple juice (from can)

~ Put the pineapple in a strainer and let it drain for 30 minutes, stirring occasionally to release juices. (Save juice for use in pineapple glaze.)
~ Combine the egg whites in a large mixing bowl and let them stand 30 minutes to bring them to room temperature.
~ Preheat the oven to 190°C/375°F/Gas Mark 5. Have ready an ungreased 25-cm/10-in ring tin.
~ Sift the flour with 175 g/6 oz sugar. Beat the egg whites until foamy. Add cream of tartar, salt and vanilla, and beat until soft peaks form. Gradually add remaining 225 g/8 oz sugar and beat until stiff peaks form. Sprinkle flour-sugar mixture over whites and gently fold in. Fold in drained pineapple.
~ Pour the mixture into ring tin. Bake until a fine skewer comes out clean, about 45 minutes. Invert cake tin and let cake cool 1 hour. Run a spatula around the rim of the cake and tin to release the cake. It will release very slowly.
~ For the glaze, combine the sugar and butter and mix well. Add the pineapple juice, a tablespoon at a time, until glaze is slightly runny. Spoon over top of cake so that it drizzles down sides.

CRANBERRY FOOL IN AN ANGEL PIE

makes 6–8 servings

We've used tart cranberries – which grow wild from the Pacific Northwest through western Canada and into Alaska – in this old-fashioned dessert. The fool, made of the fruit purée and whipped cream, can be eaten like pudding, but we've served it in an angel pie or meringue shell, made of sugar and whipped egg whites. The bright pink colour will add a festive touch to your table. Warning: the meringue shell cannot be made before the day you plan to serve it, and it will not stand up in humid weather.

350 g/12 oz fresh or frozen cranberries
about 175 g/6 oz sugar
120 ml/4 fl oz fresh orange juice
30–45 ml/2–3 tbsp orange liqueur, optional
350 ml/12 fl oz double cream

ANGEL PIE SHELL

3 large egg whites, at room temperature
⅛ tsp cream of tartar
175 g/6 oz sugar
1 tsp vanilla essence

~ Combine the cranberries, sugar and orange juice in a small saucepan. Cook over low heat until the berries split and cook down to the consistency of a thin jam. Taste. The berries should be tart, but add more sugar if they make you pucker. Cook a few minutes more to dissolve added sugar, if needed. Remove cranberries from heat. Strain through a fine-meshed sieve. Stir in the orange liqueur. Let cool to room temperature.
~ In the meantime make the case. Preheat oven to 110°C/225°F/Gas Mark ¼. Butter a 23-cm/9-in flan tin. Beat the egg whites and cream of tartar until soft peaks form. Gradually add the sugar and beat until stiff peaks form. Beat in the vanilla. Spread meringue in the buttered flan tin, building up the sides to form a shallow bowl.
~ Bake until crisp and just starting to show the first signs of browning, 1 hour or so. Do not let it brown. Turn off the oven, leave oven door ajar, and allow the meringue to cool in the oven.
~ Whip the cream until stiff. Fold in the cranberry purée. Spoon into meringue shell.

BAKED PEARS

makes 6 servings

*These baked pears are set in a nest
of filo, lightly flavoured with crystallized ginger,
and topped with an apricot glaze.
They are best served warm.*

*1 tsp ground cinnamon
3 tbsp sugar
12 sheets of filo
100 g/4 oz butter, melted
6 pears, pared, halved and cored
25 g/1 oz butter, softened to room temperature
75 g/3 oz brown sugar
1 tbsp finely chopped crystallized ginger
150 g/5 oz apricot jam or more as needed*

~ Preheat the oven to 170°C/325°F/Gas Mark 3.
~ Mix the cinnamon and sugar, if possible in a
small jar that can be used as a shaker.
~ One at a time, brush the filo sheets with melted
butter and sprinkle with the cinnamon-sugar mix.
Cut each sheet in half across its width. Line a
ramekin with a half-sheet. Add 3 more half-sheets,
each one right angles to the one under it, for a total
of four half-sheets for each cup. One layer at a
time, fold the overhanging edges back into the
ramekins so that they form a ruffled edge around
the top of the cup.
~ Mix the 25 g/1 oz butter, brown sugar and
crystallized ginger to form a paste. Put some of the
paste in the centre of each pear half and put the
halves back together. Place 1 pear in each filo nest.
~ Heat the apricot jam in a small pan until the jam
liquefies. You will need about 120 ml/4 fl oz of
syrup, strained of lumps. If the jam is a particularly
chunky variety, you may need as much as 275 g/
10 oz jam to yield 120 ml/4 fl oz of syrup. Strain
the hot jam into a measuring jug.
~ Pour some of the apricot syrup over each pear,
including a little around the edge of the filo.
~ Bake until the pears are soft and filo is golden,
about 15 minutes.

◄ *Baked Pears*

GRILLED FRUIT

makes 8 servings

*Grilling fruit caramellizes its natural sugars and brings out richer flavours.
Served warm with a soured cream-brown sugar sauce, it is delicious.*

*1 pineapple
2 bananas
2 peaches
about 75 g/3 oz brown sugar, optional
250 ml/8 fl oz soured cream
3 tbsp brown sugar
15 ml/1 tbsp orange juice*

~ Ignite the coals in a barbecue. Oil the grill.
While the coals are burning, prepare fruit
and sauce.
~ Cut the top and bottom off the pineapple.
Cut into 1-cm/$^{1}/_{2}$-in slices. Peel the slices. Peel
and cut each banana in half across its width,
then cut those halves in half lengthways. Cut
each peach into 8 wedges.

~ To make the sauce, mix the soured cream,
3 tbsp brown sugar and orange juice.
~ When the flames have died and coals are
glowing, put the fruit on grill over coals. The
bananas and peaches will be easier to cook if
they are on a rack for small items. If you don't
have a rack, put a sheet of foil over part of the
grill and punch holes in the foil to let smoke
through. Put the peach and banana slices on the
foil. Grill until edges of fruit start to brown,
2–3 minutes a side, maybe a little longer for the
pineapple. During the last minute of cooking,
sprinkle with brown sugar if desired. Remove
from grill. Serve immediately with soured cream
sauce prepared earlier.

CHERRY CUSTARD PIE

makes 8 servings

The valleys of the Pacific Northwest, from Oregon to British Columbia, produce much of North America's cherry crop. In this pie, tart cherries are paired with an almond custard.

pastry for 23-cm/9-in, double-crust pie (use double amount of tart pastry page 116)

FILLING

*3 x 450-g/1-lb. cans tart cherries
(not sweetened cherry pie filling)
225 g/8 oz sugar
2 tbsp cornflour
1 tsp flour*

CUSTARD

*75 g/3 oz sugar
1 tbsp cornflour
350 ml/12 fl oz hot milk
2 egg yolks
15 g/½ oz butter
7.5 ml/1½ tsp almond essence*

~ Roll out pastry ready, and drain the cherries. Preheat the oven to 180°C/350°F/Gas Mark 4.

~ To make the custard, mix the 75 g/3 oz sugar and 1 tbsp cornflour, then put the mixture into the top of a double saucepan with the hot milk. Heat over simmering water, stirring almost constantly, until the mixture becomes thicker.

~ Beat the egg yolks in a small bowl until they are thick and lemon-coloured. Whisk a little of the hot milk into the yolks to raise their temperature gradually. Pour the eggs into the hot milk. Heat in double saucepan, stirring constantly, until mixture thickens. Remove from heat and beat in butter and almond essence.

~ Mix the drained cherries with the 225 g/8 oz sugar and 2 tbsp cornflour. Sprinkle 1 tsp flour on pastry base. Pour the cherries into the pastry case, then pour custard over the cherries. Cover with the pastry top; seal and crimp the edges.

~ Bake until pastry is browned, 45–55 minutes.

CHOCOLATE RASPBERRY CAKE

makes 12–16 servings

This is a moist, delicious cake, with raspberries cooked into it, making a perfect marriage with the chocolate. The drizzled white and dark chocolates create a dramatic presentation.

*350 g/12 oz frozen raspberries
225 g/8 oz bittersweet or plain chocolate
unsweetened cocoa powder
225 g/8 oz butter, softened to room temperature
350 g/12 oz sugar
4 eggs
1 tsp vanilla essence
120 ml/4 fl oz milk
275 g/10 oz flour
2 tsp baking powder
¼ tsp salt
50 ml/2 fl oz raspberry liqueur, optional
100 g/4 oz white chocolate
25 g/1 oz vegetable fat
75 g/3 oz bittersweet or plain chocolate*

~ Put the raspberries in a small saucepan. Most frozen raspberries have some added sugar. If your raspberries do not, add 50 g/2 oz sugar. Cook the raspberries over low heat until they form a thick purée, 15–20 minutes. Set aside to cool.

~ Melt the 225 g/8 oz chocolate in a double saucepan or in the microwave. Set aside to cool. Preheat the oven to 170°C/325°F/Gas Mark 3. Butter a 25-cm/10-in fancy ring tin and lightly dust it with cocoa powder.

~ Cream the butter and sugar. Beat in the eggs, vanilla and milk. In a separate bowl, combine the flour, baking powder and salt. Combine the dry ingredients with the butter-egg mixture and beat until well blended. Stir in the melted chocolate, then the raspberry purée.

~ Bake until cake springs back when lightly pressed, and a fine skewer comes out clean, about 1 hour 15 minutes. Cool cake in tin, then invert and place cake on a serving plate. Drizzle the raspberry liqueur over the top, if desired, and let it soak in.

~ Melt the white chocolate and 15 g/½ oz vegetable fat in the top of a double saucepan. Warning: white chocolate is more temperamental than dark chocolate, so follow any instructions that come with the white chocolate. Remove it from heat and drizzle it over the top of the cake so it drips down the sides. Let white chocolate cool and harden before proceeding.

~ Melt the 75 g/3 oz bittersweet or plain chocolate and remaining vegetable fat. Remove chocolate from heat and let it cool about 10 minutes. Then drizzle dark chocolate over the white chocolate.

MACADAMIA SPICE BISCOTTI

makes about 24 cookies

Biscotti are an Italian biscuit, twice-baked for dryness, which makes them perfect for dunking in coffee or dessert wine. Traditionally they are not too sweet and are flavoured with anise, but as they've caught on in the United States, biscuit lovers have demanded sweeter, more varied biscotti. These biscotti are flavoured with cinnamon and ginger and studded with roasted macadamia nuts. They are also made with butter, which makes them a little softer than traditional biscotti.

75 g/3 oz macadamia nuts
100 g/4 oz butter, softened
175 g/6 oz sugar
2 eggs
5 ml/1 tsp vanilla essence
225 g/8 oz flour
1½ tsp baking powder
¼ tsp salt
1 tsp ground cinnamon
½ tsp ground ginger

~ Preheat the oven to 180°C/350°F/Gas Mark 4. Grease a large baking sheet or line it with foil.

~ Coarsely chop the nuts into 3 or 4 pieces each. Put them on a small baking sheet and roast them until they start to brown, about 10 minutes. Set them aside to cool.

~ In a large bowl, cream the butter and sugar. Beat in the eggs and vanilla. In a separate bowl, combine the dry ingredients. Mix dry ingredients with butter-sugar mixture, kneading by hand if necessary. Mix in the chopped macadamia nuts.

~ Form the dough into 2 logs, 4–5 cm/1½–2 in wide, and 25–30 cm/10–12 in long. Place on baking sheet and bake until logs are lightly browned and still slightly soft, about 25 minutes. Remove them from the oven and reduce temperature to 150°C/300°F/Gas Mark 2. Let the logs cool about 15 minutes. On a slight diagonal, slice the logs into biscuits about 2 cm/³/₄ in thick. Put them back on the baking sheet and cook about 15 minutes more, until they are hard and colour is just starting to darken.

~ Put them on a wire rack to cool. Store them in an airtight container.

TAHITIAN BANANA FRITTERS

makes 6 servings

Sometimes we forget how versatile the banana is. Here it becomes a delicious dessert, dipped in batter and fried, then sprinkled with icing sugar. For an extra treat, serve the fritters with whipped cream that has been flavoured with rum or rum flavouring.

100 g/4 oz flour
1½ tsp baking powder
¼ tsp salt
1 egg, beaten
3 tbsp sugar
120 ml/4 fl oz milk
15 g/½ oz butter, melted
oil for deep-frying
4 bananas, cut into 4-cm/1½-inch pieces
icing sugar

~ Mix the flour, baking powder and salt. In a separate bowl, mix egg, sugar, milk and butter. Combine with dry ingredients. If you have time, leave the batter to stand in the refrigerator for an hour or so.

~ Pour oil into a frying pan to a depth of 5 cm/ 2 in. Heat oil. Dip the bananas into the batter.

~ When the temperature of the oil has reached 180°C/360°F, reduce the heat and carefully put several fritters into the oil. Fry until golden, turning once, about 3 minutes a side. Let drain on kitchen paper towels and sprinkle with icing sugar while still hot. Fritters can be kept warm in the oven while the rest are cooking, if desired. Make sure oil temperature has returned to 180°C/360°F before cooking each batch.

GLOSSARY

FISH

From the fishing villages of western Mexico to the mighty rivers of California and Washington, from frigid Alaskan waters to warm Hawaiian currents, the hallmark of Ocean Pacific cooking is seafood. The Pacific Ocean and the rivers that feed it nurture a tremendous variety of seafood.

Trout

Mussels

Salmon

SALMON

There are five varieties of Pacific salmon, ranging as far south as San Francisco and the spawning grounds of Northern California's Sacramento River, and as far north as the Arctic Circle. Unlike commercial Atlantic salmon, most of which are pen-reared, Pacific salmon are fished from the rivers of the north Pacific. The most popular varieties are King salmon, also known as chinook, spring or Columbia River salmon, which are large and have a high fat content; and the smaller but similarly rich sockeye, also known as red or blueback salmon. The King salmon, a favourite game fish because of its size, can be as large as 57 kg/125 lb, although most commercially caught fish are 4.5–13.5 kg/10–30 lb. The sockeye is less plentiful and runs to about 2.75 kg/6 lb. Its landlocked version, the kokanee, is also a delicious sport fish. The pink or humpback salmon is the most plentiful and most of the commercial catch is canned. The pink is the smallest and least oily salmon, averaging 1–2.25 kg/2–5 lb. The silver or coho salmon, which ranges from 1.75–5.5kg/4–12 lb, is fished commercially and for sport. The chum or dog salmon is of the lowest quality, but because it ranges farther north than other salmon, is an important staple in Alaska, where it is often smoked or dried. Salmon is also popular in Hawaii, where it is farm-raised. All salmon are high-fat fish, and can be used interchangeably in most recipes.

HALIBUT

A favourite sport fish, the halibut lives in deep, cold water. It is most commonly associated with Alaska, although it may range as far south as the waters off Northern California. A smaller variety is caught off the Southern California coast. The halibut is a giant flatfish, low in fat and with firm-textured flesh. Its usual range is 2–27 kg/5–60 lb, although Alaskan halibut can be as much as 228 kg/500 lb.

TUNA

There are five major varieties of tuna, an oily fish caught off Mexico, Southern California and Hawaii. The largest is the bluefin, which can weight as much as 450 kg/1000 lb. The smallest and least fatty is the bonito, which rarely exceeds 2.25 kg/5 lb. Albacore, the only tuna that can be called white-meat tuna, runs from 4.5–36 kg/10–80 lb and is called tombo in Hawaii. The yellowfin, weighing 13.5–115kg/30–250 lb, is called ahi in Hawaii. The highest grade of ahi, with a deeper red colour and higher fat content, is often used in sashimi. Skipjack, called aku in Hawaii, has a bolder taste than ahi, and generally runs between 2.25–11.25 kg/5–25 lb.

SNAPPER

The plentiful rockfish is often sold as Pacific snapper, although it is not related to the Atlantic Ocean's popular red snapper. There are more than 50 varieties of Pacific snapper, but they are generally low-fat, firm-textured fish of 0.5–2.25 kg/1–5 lb. The Hawaiian red snapper, also known as onaga, may range as large as 8.25 kg/18 lb and is often used in sashimi. Opakapaka is a Hawaiian pink snapper of 0.5–5.5 kg/1–12 lb.

MAHI MAHI

Mahi mahi is the Hawaiian name for dolphin fish, which is not the same as the dolphin mammal. Mahi mahi frequents the warm waters of the world. It averages 3.5–18 kg/8–40 lb, and has firm-textured flesh with a moderate fat content.

OTHER FISH

Other fish frequently used in Pacific Rim cooking are the **ono** or **wahoo**, a member of the mackerel family with lean, mild-flavoured flesh similar to the albacore; **swordfish**, which has a dense, meat-like texture and is caught in the Pacific and Atlantic oceans and the Gulf of Mexico; **shark**, with a flavour and dense texture similar to swordfish; **sablefish** or **black cod**, a small, high-fat, soft-textured Alaskan fish that is often smoked; **Pacific cod**, unrelated to black cod, is a low-fat fish similar to the Atlantic cod, but runs a little smaller, about 2.25–4.5 kg/5–10 lb; and **trout**, typically the small Rainbow trout, which is commercially farmed but can be fished in mountain streams and lakes from California to Alaska.

SHELLFISH

CRAB

~~~~~~~~~~~~~~~~~~~~~~~~~~~~~~~

Dungeness crab, harvested from the San Francisco Bay to the Aleutian Islands, generally runs from 0.5–1.5 kg/1–3 lb. It is large and meaty, and was the inspiration for cioppino, a Pacific seafood stew. It is similar in size to Florida's golden crab. Alaska's enormous King crab averages 4.5 kg/10 lb, with a leg span of 1.2–1.8 m/4–6 ft. The meat is snow white with red edges, and is mostly in the legs, with relatively little in the body. The north Pacific's snow crab, a little larger than Dungeness, is known for its sweet flavour. Kona crabs from Hawaii are also very sweet. Although sizes of crabs vary tremendously, and different varieties have subtle differences in flavour, you can generally substitute equal amounts of shelled meat of one crab variety for another.

MUSSELS

~~~~~~~~~~~~~~~~~~~~~~~~~~~~~~~

The under-appreciated mussel is plentiful along the Pacific Coast, where it attaches itself to rocks and pilings along the beach. Most mussels are caught wild, but they are increasingly being farmed, from New Zealand to the Pacific Northwest. Sweet, tender California mussels are smaller than the more common Atlantic mussel. In Alaska, the wild blue mussel is considered a gourmet treat.

PRAWNS

~~~~~~~~~~~~~~~~~~~~~~~~~~~~~~~

The Pacific Ocean supports dozens of varieties of saltwater prawns, which are fished – and occasionally farmed – from Mexico to Alaska, and from Hawaii to the South Pacific. Alaska's commercial catch has five major species, from the spot prawns, which can grow to 30 cm/12 in, to the cocktail-sized pink prawns. Fresh and saltwater Kahuku prawns are farmed in Hawaii. Mexico has thousands of miles of coastline where prawns – camarones – are plentiful, and lakes that produce freshwater prawns.

CLAMS

~~~~~~~~~~~~~~~~~~~~~~~~~~~~~~~

Clam-digging, although not as popular as it was when coastal communities were less populated, is still done along the beaches of the western United States. Alaska alone has more than 160 species of clams. Clams are farmed in Hawaii. Manila clams, also marketed as littleneck clams, are the Pacific's most common hard-shell clam. Butter, Pismo, horseneck, cockle and razor clams are other Pacific hard-shell varieties. In the Pacific Northwest, the huge and ugly geoduck clam is the star. It is called a soft-shell clam, although it really has a thin, brittle shell that cannot close completely because the clam spills out of the shell. The geoduck averages about 1.5 kg/3 lb, with part sold as clam steak and tougher sections used in chowder.

OYSTERS

~~~~~~~~~~~~~~~~~~~~~~~~~~~~~~~

The Pacific oyster, transplanted from Japan to the coastal waters of the western United States in the 1920s, is the main oyster cultivated in U.S. and Canadian Pacific oyster beds today. It is typically sold under the name of the bay where it was grown, such as the Willapa Bay oyster from Willapa Bay, Oregon. The only oyster native to Pacific waters is the Olympia oyster, which once thrived in beds from Mexico to Alaska. This tiny, sweet oyster was over-harvested, and today is found only in Washington's Puget Sound. Oysters are also farmed in Alaska, but they do not grow as plentifully in the icy water as they do farther south.

OTHER SHELLFISH

~~~~~~~~~~~~~~~~~~~~~~~~~~~~~~~

Crawfish, usually associated with Louisiana cooking, grow wild in California's Sacramento River and the rivers of the Pacific Northwest. Pacific **scallops** include the Weathervane, a large sea scallop found from Oregon to Alaska; the very small Oregon bay scallop, found in that state's coastal bays; and the singing scallop, found offshore from Washington and British Columbia.

Crab

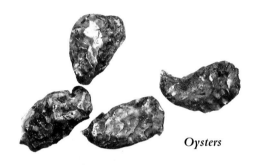

Oysters

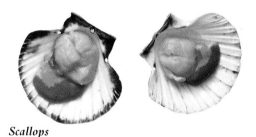

Scallops

Shrimp

PRODUCE – FRUIT

Lime

Pineapple

Mango

CITRUS FRUIT

~~~~~~~~~~~~~~~~~~~~~~~~~~~~~~

Many citrus fruits are valuable not only for eating plain or as juice, but for the flavour they add to other dishes. Citrus juices are excellent in salsas, meat marinades and salad dressings. They perk up bland vegetables and fish, and are delicious in desserts. Orange, grapefruit and lime juice are often mixed into cocktails. The grated rind of oranges and lemons, and to a lesser extent limes, add flavour to rice, breads and desserts. Generally when looking for citrus fruit, look for a smooth skin, no sign of shrivelling, and a heavy weight that suggests a high juice content. Much of the nation's citrus crop is grown at the southern end of California's San Joaquin Valley, and in some parts of Southern California that have not been urbanized.

PINEAPPLES

~~~~~~~~~~~~~~~~~~~~~~~~~~~~~~

The pineapple, grown on sprawling Hawaiian plantations, is native to the West Indies. It made its way to Hawaii in the early 1800s via South America. Delicious plain, pineapple also pairs well with pork and fish, rice, curries, salsas, and in desserts. Pineapples do not ripen after they are picked. Check for a sweet fragrance. A lack of aroma means it is not sweet; a sour or winey smell means it is overripe and fermenting.

MANGOES

~~~~~~~~~~~~~~~~~~~~~~~~~~~~~~

The mango, native to the Himalayas, is a tropical fruit widely grown in Hawaii, Tahiti and Mexico, as well as Florida and non-Pacific locales. There are nearly 500 varieties of mango, dating back more than 4,000 years, when they played an important part in religious ceremonies in India. The mango is a smooth-skinned, oval fruit that can range in size a great deal. Its sweet, juicy flesh is often used in salsas, chutneys, meat marinades, salads and desserts. Hawaiians season the green, unripe mango with vinegar and soy sauce and eat it like a vegetable. Because of the many varieties, colour is not a good indicator of ripeness. Look for unwrinkled skin, a sweet smell and firm flesh. Unripe mangoes, if not too green, will ripen in your kitchen in a few days.

Take care when handling mangoes, though: they are related to poison ivy, and the peel will irritate some people's skin.

PEACHES, APRICOTS AND OTHER STONE FRUIT

~~~~~~~~~~~~~~~~~~~~~~~~~~~~~~

Most of the nation's stone fruits – peaches, plums, nectarines, apricots and cherries – are grown on the West Coast, and much of that in California. About 60 percent of the nation's peaches and 97 percent of its apricots are grown in California's Central Valley. Washington, Oregon and British Columbia – particularly their eastern regions, where summers are hotter – are also major producers of stone fruits. Because of shipping requirements, these fruits are often shipped unripe. If they are close, the fruit can be ripened in the kitchen or in paper bags. But others become mealy or were picked so green that they never develop juice or sweetness. Look for farmers' markets or buy the fruit as close to the source as possible.

BERRIES

~~~~~~~~~~~~~~~~~~~~~~~~~~~~~~

Berries are fragile, with a short shelf-life. Once ripe, they spoil quickly if not eaten. On the other hand, too many berries, especially strawberries, are picked unripe. But what a treat when they are fresh-picked and perfectly ripe! In general, look for plump, juicy berries that are no longer hard, but have not turned mushy. Store them, unwashed, in the refrigerator.

Blueberries love the long, cool summers of the Pacific Northwest, particularly along the coast and valleys west of the Cascades, through Canada and even into Alaska. They wear a sort of frosted blush at their peak. When that whitish blush fades, they are past their prime.

The red **raspberry**, native to Europe, was introduced to North America in the early 1800s and now grows abundantly in cooler climates, as far north as Alaska. More than 90 percent of North America's commercial raspberry crop comes from Oregon, Washington and British Columbia. The most common variety is the Willamette, named for the Oregon valley where it thrives.

Blackberries grow wild in Northern California, Oregon and Washington, while cultivated varieties include the sweet Marion berry, the tart loganberry, and the boysenberry, a hybrid of the wild blackberry, loganberry and raspberry. Oregon is the world's largest producer of commercial blackberries.

Strawberries, first cultivated in France as shrubs, were brought to the U.S. in 1835. There are now about 75 varieties grown in the U.S., and California is the No. 1 producer. Commercial varieties grown in the Pacific Northwest include the Hood, Benton, Olympus, and Totem. Hawaii has large Waimea strawberries. Small Yukon and beach strawberries grow in Alaska.

Huckleberries, closely related to blueberries, grow wild in the Pacific Northwest, where they were a staple food of American Indians.

Cranberries – Because so much of the commercial cranberry crop comes from the New England states, many people don't realize that the cranberry grows wild in the Pacific Coast too, from Alaska to the coastal bogs and mountain meadows of Oregon. American Indians harvested them before white settlers came. Finnish settlers along the Washington coast later began commercial cultivation of cranberries.

Once a more popular fruit, **gooseberries** have fallen out of favour. Today, these tart, pale green berries are grown commercially only in Oregon. Gooseberries are related to the **tomatillo**, a small, green fruit that looks like a small tomato with a papery husk. Tomatillos are commonly used in Mexican salsas and other sauces. Less common berries include lingonberries, salmonberries, nagoonberries and cloudberries.

GRAPES
~~~~~~~~~~~~~~~~~~~~~~~~~~~~~~~~

Thousands of acres in California's San Joaquin Valley are planted with sweet, green-gold Thompson seedless grapes, the premier table grape. In the autumn, large bunches of grapes are spread on paper trays and left to dry in the sun between rows of grapevines, where they turn into raisins. The small farm towns around Fresno fight to be called Raisin Capital of the World. In addition to being eaten plain or in biscuits and baked goods, raisins add just the right touch of sweetness to savoury dishes such as meat fillings in Mexican empanadas, or rice casseroles.

CHERRIES
~~~~~~~~~~~~~~~~~~~~~~~~~~~~~~~~

Cherries love hot summers, so orchards are planted from California's San Joaquin Valley, through the Willamette, Hood, Yakima and Wenatchee Valleys of Oregon and Washington, to British Columbia's Okanagan Valley. The most common sweet varieties are the Bing and Lambert, and for cooking or canning, the yellow Rainier. The yellow-skinned Royal Ann is made into maraschino cherries. Sour cherries, also called tart or pie cherries, are also grown in the Pacific Northwest. They do not have a good flavour if eaten raw, but are the star of pies. Some people substitute sweet cherries for tart, cut the sugar and add a little lemon, but I think pies made with sweet cherries are insipid.

PAPAYAS
~~~~~~~~~~~~~~~~~~~~~~~~~~~~~~~~

The pear-shaped papaya has a sweet, delicate flavour and an orange or rosy pulp, depending on the variety. It is a tropical fruit grown in Hawaii and Mexico. Most commonly it is eaten with a splash of lime juice. It can also be an ingredient in salsa or other sauces. Hawaiians eat the green, unripe papaya as a vegetable, similar to squash. Although there are many varieties, the main commercial variety has a bright yellow-orange skin when ripe. Papayas, if not too green, will ripen in your kitchen after a few days.

BANANAS
~~~~~~~~~~~~~~~~~~~~~~~~~~~~~~~~

Bananas are the most popular fruit in the United States, which consumed 7.5 billion pounds of them in 1993. Most come from Central and South America, but Mexico is also a big producer. The bananas that grow in Hawaii today were transplanted from Polynesia. There are about 100 varieties of bananas, with the Cavendish being the most widely popular. Bananas are closely related to plantains, starchy fruit that are cooked and eaten like vegetables.

Blueberries

Papaya

Cherries

Banana

Apples

Strawberries

Pears

Coconut

APPLES

~~~~~~~~~~~~~~~~~~~~~~~~~~~~~~~~

Washington, Oregon, California and British Columbia produce dozens of varieties of apples, from the sweet Golden Delicious to the tart Newton-Pippin. Sixty percent of the nation's commercial fresh apple crop comes from Washington, with different varieties coming from the milder climate west of the Cascades, and the hotter region to the East. Apples also do well in the valleys of Oregon and British Columbia and the Sierra foothills of Northern California. The Red and Golden Delicious are excellent fresh fruit, but are not good cooking apples, except for making apple purée. The McIntosh of British Columbia, Newton-Pippin, Jonathan, Winesap, Rome Beauty and Gravenstein are better cooking apples.

PEARS

~~~~~~~~~~~~~~~~~~~~~~~~~~~~~~~~

Bartlett pears like intense summer heat, and do well in central California and the foothills of the Sierra Nevada, as well as in parts of Oregon and Washington. Bartletts, the only summer pear, are also the most well known. Most canned pears are Bartletts. But winter pears – including the russet-skinned Bosc, Anjou, Comice, and the tiny Seckel or sugar pear – are also delicious and can be substituted in most recipes calling for pear. Ninety-five percent of the nation's winter pear crop is grown in Oregon and Washington.

NUTS

~~~~~~~~~~~~~~~~~~~~~~~~~~~~~~~~

Ocean Pacific cooking features a variety of nuts whose uses are not limited to biscuits. Nuts are excellent in salads, with fish, in rice dishes, sprinkled over cooked vegetables, and ground up in spreads and pâtés. Nuts keep best when refrigerated, but should be stored in an airtight container so they do not absorb refrigerator odours. Nuts left at room temperature may turn rancid within a few months. Roasting nuts heightens their flavour. To roast nuts, spread them in a single layer on a baking sheet and cook in a 180°C/350°F/Gas Mark 4 oven for 5–15 minutes, depending on their size and type. They must be monitored carefully, as they go quickly from nicely toasted to scorched. To remove the inner skins of roasted hazelnuts and pistachios, rub the shelled nuts against each other in a coarse towel. To remove the inner skins of uncooked almonds, hazelnuts and filberts, pour boiling water over them, let sit for a minute, then drain and rub off the skins.

Almonds, related to apricots, are grown in Central California. Almonds are perhaps the most versatile nut, playing a lead role in dishes from Trout Amandine to marzipan. They are also good in salads, rice and vegetable dishes, as a coating for fish, and ground up and baked in tortes.

Hazelnuts, almost identical in flavour to the European filbert, are often roasted and ground and used in desserts. They pair wonderfully with chocolate. Wild hazelnuts were an important winter food to American Indians of the Pacific Northwest. Today Oregon's Willamette Valley produces most of the nation's commercial hazelnut crop, with Washington and British Columbia producing the rest.

Macadamia nuts from Australia were introduced to Hawaii in 1892. The nut has a rich, buttery flavour, and is usually available on the mainland only salted and roasted. Macadamia nuts may be added to salads, rice, fish and desserts.

Pistachio nuts from California, usually eaten roasted and salted, are also excellent in spreads and pâtés.

Walnuts are almost as versatile as the almond. They are excellent in salads and spreads, as a substitute for expensive pine nuts in pesto, and in desserts. Eaten plain, they pair wonderfully with red wines and strong cheeses, such as sharp Cheddar, goats' and blue cheeses. California is the main grower of walnuts, which are more common and have a much different flavour than the South's scarcer black walnut.

COCONUTS

~~~~~~~~~~~~~~~~~~~~~~~~~~~~~~~~

The coconut was introduced to Hawaii by Polynesians. It produces a creamy milk often used in Thai and Southeast Asian cooking. Its hard white flesh is flaked or grated and used in curries, seafood dishes and desserts. Most prepackaged flaked coconut is sweetened for dessert use.

VEGETABLES

TOMATOES
~~~~~~~~~~~~~~~~~~~~~~~~~~~~~~~

Tomatoes love the hot summers of California's Sacramento Valley, which produces much of the nation's crop. Sacramento, mindful of its role as centre of the tomato-processing industry as well as the state capital of California, sometimes calls itself Sacratomato. Unfortunately, tomatoes travel poorly, which means they are often shipped to market hard and flavourless. Put unripe tomatoes in a paper bag for a few days, and they may ripen. However, if they were picked too green (you can't tell by the colour because they are often gassed to turn them red prematurely), they may spoil before they ripen. Truly ripe tomatoes have a sweet tomato smell. Look for them at farmers' markets or grow your own to get the best flavour. Canned tomatoes are a good substitute in cooked dishes. Small but meaty Roma tomatoes may be shipped riper than other varieties. Sun-dried tomatoes, a trademark of California's nouvelle cuisine, add a tart flavour and a chewy texture to salads, soups, pastas and sauces.

LETTUCES AND SALAD GREENS
~~~~~~~~~~~~~~~~~~~~~~~~~~~~~~~

Iceberg has long been the king of salads, but people are increasingly looking for alternatives to its bland flavour. In addition to more varieties of lettuce, many supermarkets also carry blends of wild and domestic lettuces, usually called mesclun. These blends typically include a mix of sweet and bitter, tender and crisp. Among the most popular lettuces are the closely related **Bibb** and **Boston** lettuce, with tender, buttery leaves; **loose-leaf** lettuces, including oak leaf and red leaf, with tender, mild leaves; **Cos**, the backbone of Caesar Salad, with long, stiff, dark green leaves, crunchy white ribs, and a somewhat stronger flavour; **arugula** or **rocket**, a red-leafed lettuce with a pronounced flavour popular in Italian cuisine; **chicory** or **curly endive**, with spiky leaves and a bitter flavour; **Belgian endive**, whose bitter, blanched-white leaves may be stuffed or dipped like celery or crackers; **watercress**, with a peppery flavour; **mâche** or **lamb's lettuce**, with small, bland leaves; and **radicchio**, with a slightly bitter flavour and purplish-red leaves with white

veins. In Alaska, young **dandelion greens, fireweed, lamb's quarters, sorrel, goose tongue, chickweed** and **beach green** are added to salad, or cooked like spinach or turnip greens. One delicacy among greens is the **fiddlehead fern**, the tender, curled fronds of certain edible ferns including bracken, ostrich and cinnamon ferns. Most often these sweet, crunchy young leaves are eaten raw in salad or steamed. They are very popular in Canada, and can also be found in Alaska, Washington and Hawaii, where they are called pohole.

ASPARAGUS
~~~~~~~~~~~~~~~~~~~~~~~~~~~~~~~

Long a delicacy in Europe, asparagus is also a favourite in the U.S. Central California is a major asparagus producer, with a large crop from February to early summer, and a smaller fall crop. Imported asparagus is available most of the rest of the year. Although the thinnest stalks are often an aesthetic favourite, they are no more tender than fat stalks. Look for firm, unshrivelled spears with tightly budded tips.

BROCCOLI
~~~~~~~~~~~~~~~~~~~~~~~~~~~~~~~

Although broccoli has been cultivated in Europe for centuries, this member of the cabbage family was not commercially grown in the U.S. until the 1920s. Today it is a major crop in the Salinas Valley and the cooler regions of California, which grows about 90 percent of the nation's crop. Mexico also produces a large broccoli crop, as does Oregon's Willamette Valley.

ARTICHOKES
~~~~~~~~~~~~~~~~~~~~~~~~~~~~~~~

The odd-looking globe artichoke is actually a flower and a member of the thistle family. The canned artichoke hearts sold in supermarkets are actually trimmed baby artichokes. Ninety-nine percent of American artichokes come from California, 75 percent of them from Castroville, the self-proclaimed Artichoke Capital of the World, near the coast of Central California. Look for bright green artichokes with tightly packed leaves and use before the leaf tips have the chance to dry out.

Dandelion

Chicory

Broccoli

Romaine

Garlic

Spring onions

Ginger

Onion

GARLIC

~~~~~~~~~~~~~~~~~~~~~~~~~~~~~~~~

Garlic is easily grown in home gardens, but the biggest commercial production is in Gilroy, California, a coastal community south of San Francisco. Every year, Gilroy holds a Garlic Festival, the highlight of which is the cooking and tasting of garlic dishes, from garlic soup to garlic ice cream. Long valued for its sharp flavour and aroma, garlic has only recently drawn wide appreciation for the mellowing that occurs when garlic is roasted. When sautéing garlic, cook it only briefly, until it begins to brown. It scorches easily, becoming bitter. Look for heads of garlic with large, solid cloves that have not begun to wither.

ONIONS

~~~~~~~~~~~~~~~~~~~~~~~~~~~~~~~

Onions are a crucial ingredient in Pacific Rim cooking and there are many varieties to choose from. The most common are the dry, globe onions, including the yellow and white **Bermudas**, and the milder, flat **Spanish** and elongated **Italian red**. Sweet, mild globe onions with a high sugar content include the **Maui** onion from Hawaii and the **Walla Walla Sweet** from Washington, similar to Georgia's Vidalia onion. Some people swear they are so sweet they can be eaten like apples. I prefer them sliced raw in salads, grilled or roasted. **Spring onions**, the thinnings of globe onions, add strong flavour and crunch to salsas, salads, and – when added at the end of cooking – to soups, stews and bean dishes. **Leeks**, with their narrow, elongated white roots and tough green tops, add a wonderful, delicate flavour to soups. Thin stalks of **chives**, used as a herb, give food a pungent, aromatic accent. Finely chopped **shallots** give an excellent flavour to cooked sauces.

GINGER

~~~~~~~~~~~~~~~~~~~~~~~~~~~~~~~~

Ginger is a rhizome or underground stem with a hot, pungent yet slightly sweet flavour. It thrives under tropical conditions, and grows profusely in Hawaii. Ginger is widely used in Hawaiian, Asian, Mexican and North American cooking, seasoning everything from drinks and soups to fish and dessert. Fresh ginger root and dried ground ginger are the most common

forms, but it is also crystallized in sugar as candy or an ingredient in Chinese sweets, or pickled and used as a sushi condiment. When buying fresh ginger, look for pieces with thin, unwrinkled skin. It can be stored in the refrigerator for about two weeks.

JICAMA

~~~~~~~~~~~~~~~~~~~~~~~~~~~~~~~

Jicama is an ugly-duckling vegetable, a misshapen brown bulb. But the tuber has a crisp, slightly sweet, ivory-coloured flesh that is excellent eaten raw as crudités, in salads, steamed or boiled. It can be substituted for water chestnuts in stir-fries. In Mexico, jicama sticks are eaten raw with a splash of lime juice and a sprinkling of salt and chilli powder. Look for smooth, thin-skinned jicama, and keep it in the refrigerator.

AVOCADOS

~~~~~~~~~~~~~~~~~~~~~~~~~~~~~~~~

Nearly 500 varieties of avocado are grown in tropical climates. The two types most commonly available in the U.S. are the Haas, which is oilier and more flavourful, and is distinguishable by its black, bumpy skin; and the Fuerte, which has only half the oil content of the Fuerte and less flavour, and has smooth, green skin. The Haas avocado, grown in California, is available in late spring through early autumn, while the Fuerte, grown in Florida, is available during the winter. Look for avocados that are firm, not soft. It is rare to find them perfectly ripe in the store, so plan ahead, buy them when they are still hard, and ripen them in a paper bag. Do not refrigerate them until they are perfectly ripe.

MUSHROOMS

~~~~~~~~~~~~~~~~~~~~~~~~~~~~~~~~

More than 3,000 varieties of wild mushrooms thrive in the cool, moist climate of the Pacific Northwest, particularly in the Cascade Mountains of Oregon and Washington. Most are not edible, but among the delicious varieties that can be eaten are the shitake, oyster, morel, chanterelle, porcini and matsutake. Alaska has more than 500 species of wild mushrooms. The most common are the puffball, morel, shaggy mane, and chicken of the woods.

CHILLIES AND PEPPERS

Chillies are mostly used as seasoning, to add heat to dishes, but larger varieties such as the Anaheim and poblano are often stuffed with cheese, bean or meat fillings. Chillies are distinguished by their level of heat, which comes from capsaicin, a compound concentrated near the stem in the placenta and veins. In addition to adding heat to food, the capsaicin will irritate your skin, so protect your fingers with rubber gloves or even a plastic bag when you handle them.

The most common varieties of fresh chillies, from mildest to hottest, are the **Anaheim** or **California chilli**, a long, skinny, relatively flat green chilli that is often roasted and peeled, and is good for stuffing, it is the variety most frequently canned; the **poblano**, moderately spicy, black-green and triangular with wide shoulders like a pepper but narrowing to a tip, it is rarely eaten raw but is usually roasted and peeled, then stuffed or chopped; the **jalapeño**, probably the most widely available chilli in the U.S. and the one most people consider a hot chilli, smooth and usually 7.5–10 cm/3–4 in long, it is mostly available green, but turns red if it is allowed to ripen, it is also available pickled or smoked (as chipotle); the **serrano**, smaller and

hotter than the jalapeño, usually chopped raw into salsas, it is sold both in its green and red stages; the **Hawaiian** chilli, a small red or yellow chilli that is fiery hot; the Thai **bird's eye** chilli, tiny, red or green and very hot; and the Mexican **habanero** and Caribbean **Scotch Bonnet**, the hottest chillies in the world, sold green, orange and red, the habanero looks like a miniature pepper, while the Scotch Bonnet looks like a puffy tam-o'-shanter.

Dried chillies are frequently used in Mexican cooking. They are soaked in hot water, then puréed to make enchilada sauce or an addition to soups and stews. The most common dried chillies, from mildest to hottest, are the **California**; the **ancho**, the dried form of the poblano; the **jalapeño**, or in its smoked form, the **chipotle**; the **New Mexico**; and the **chilli de arbol**, usually a dried serrano, but it may be any other small, very hot chilli.

Although related to chillies, **peppers** have no capsaicin and cannot be substituted for chillies. Allowed to ripen on the plant, peppers turn sweet and bright red. The red pepper is often roasted and peeled and adds a marvellous flavour to soups, sauces and vegetable dishes.

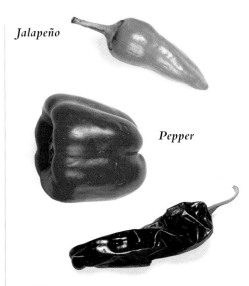

Jalapeño

Pepper

California

Chillies are cultivated and used in cooking around the world, from the Italian sweet chilli to the fiery Thai chilli and the Caribbean's incendiary Scotch Bonnet. But Mexico grows more varieties and puts them to greater use than any other country.

LENTILS AND DRIED BEANS

Lentils are grown worldwide, but most of North America's lentils and dried peas are grown in the Palouse region of eastern Washington and Oregon and Idaho. Lentils are available in more than 50 varieties. Although a member of the dried bean family, they do not require soaking and cook in as little as 15 minutes, depending on how they are processed. The other dried bean that is a current staple of Ocean Pacific cooking is the **black bean** or **turtle bean**, usually associated with Mexican and Southwestern cooking. Black beans have a nutty, smokey flavour, and are wonderful in soups, salads, stuffed in chillies or enchiladas, in huevos rancheros, or simply simmered with onions and spices. Other beans frequently used in Ocean Pacific cooking are the **red kidney bean** and the light brown **pinto bean**, the bean most often used in Mexican refried beans.

RICE

Much of the nation's **white rice** is grown in California's Sacramento Valley. White rice is polished to remove its bran coat. Long-grain white rice, when cooked, tends to produce fluffy, separate grains. Medium-grain and short-grain white rice tend to be sticky, making them ideal for eating with chopsticks. **Brown rice**, with its bran coat and germ intact, has a nutty flavour, more nutrients than white rice, and takes longer to cook. **Wild rice** is not really a rice, but the seed of a grass that grows wild at the edges of lakes in Minnesota and Wisconsin, and is cultivated in Northern California. Wild rice is expensive, nutty and chewy. Two exotic rices that are gaining attention in Pacific Rim cooking are **basmati**, an aromatic rice from India, and **arborio**, an Italian rice is used in risottos.

A selection of pulses including kidney beans, black-eyed peas and various lentils.

HERBS AND SPICES

Sorrel

Lemongrass

Chives

Fresh herbs make a wonderful addition to almost any dish and can turn something plain and boring – simple grilled fish, mashed potatoes, steamed vegetables – into something delicious. As a rule of thumb, use three times as much fresh herb as dried, because the flavour is more concentrated in dried herbs. Rosemary, with its potent flavour, is one exception – I use only twice as much fresh. Some herbs, including coriander, lemongrass and tarragon, lose much of their flavour when dried, and should only be used fresh. These are some of the herbs most commonly used in Pacific Rim cooking.

Coriander, also known as **cilantro** or **Chinese parsley**, is a staple of Mexican and Southeast Asian cooking. It is a member of the parsley family with a pungent flavour that goes well in soups, bean dishes and salsas. Look for bunches with bright green leaves, preferably with the roots still attached, and keep in the refrigerator with a wet kitchen paper towel wrapped around the roots. Ground coriander seed is widely used in curries, but is not interchangeable with fresh coriander.

Basil is a staple in Italian and Southeast Asian cooking, where it is often paired with mint. It is the star ingredient in traditional pesto, and goes wonderfully with tomatoes. An annual, it is easy to grow in herb gardens. Any excess can be made into pesto, then frozen for winter use. There are many varieties of basil, some with flavours such as lemon, but sweet basil is the common variety.

Oregano is a sweet, mild herb often used in Italian and other Mediterranean cuisines. Mexican oregano is sometimes added to salsa and other Mexican sauces. Oregano is much more potent in its dried form, and can easily dominate a dish. If fresh oregano is not available, choose the dried leaf over the powdered form.

Thyme is another assertive herb often used in Mediterranean cooking, but which goes well with a greater variety of meat, poultry, fish, soups and stews.

Dill, increasingly available fresh, is wonderful with fish. It is a staple in Russian and Scandinavian cooking, and is often found in immigrant communities in Alaska and Washington. Dill seed has a different taste and should not be substituted for fresh or dried dillweed.

Fragrant, piney **rosemary** gives a Mediterranean flavour to meats and other dishes, but should be used sparingly because of its potency. I like to roast potatoes with rosemary and use it in focaccia.

Tarragon, a delicate herb with hints of lemon and licorice, is excellent with fish, veal, eggs and salad dressing, and is the signature seasoning in béarnaise sauce. It loses most of its flavour when dried.

Lemongrass, widely used in Asian cooking, has a pungent lemon perfume. It grows in tall stalks; only the tender inner shoots should be mixed into a dish. The coarse outer leaves can be added to soups and stews, then removed, like a bay leaf. Although dried lemongrass is available, it loses most of its lemony fragrance and has more of a peppery taste.

Vanilla – the vanilla plant, a member of the orchid family, produces a long, thin bean filled with tiny seeds and pulpy flesh. After harvesting, the vanilla bean is fermented until it is dark brown. It is most commonly used to flavour ice cream and other desserts. It is cultivated in Tahiti and Mexico.

Chilli powder is either a commercial seasoning mix of ground mild chillies and other spices or a powder of pure ground chillies, with the heat depending on the type of chilli used. **Cayenne** is usually pure ground cayenne chillies, the hottest of powdered chillies, but may be the generic name for other hot ground chillies. Because chilli powders vary so widely, add very sparingly to a dish until the desired degree of heat is reached.

Cumin seed, native to the Mediterranean, has a pungent, aromatic flavour. The ground seed is used in Mexican cooking, as well as in the Middle East and India, where it is an ingredient in curries. Cumin goes well with meats and beans.